P9-EJU-340

mother of jesus present with us

by paul hinnebusch, o. p.

From the Library of:
Jehane Jones

PROW BOOKS

1600 W. Park Avenue
Libertyville, IL 60048

Imprimi Potest:

Very Rev. Gerard B. Cleator, O.P.

Imprimatur:

†Thomas Tschoepe
Bishop of Dallas
May 18, 1978

Copyright © 1980 by Paul Hinnebusch

Library of Congress Catalog Card Number: 79-93231

ISBN 0-913382-32-9

Biblical quotations are from the Revised Standard Version
Bible, Catholic Edition, copyrighted © 1965 and 1966 by the
Division of Christian Eduacation of the National Council of
the Churches of Christ in the U.S.A., and used by permission.

contents

O Mary, Mother of God,
I dedicate this book to you,
who appeared to the Mexican Indian Juan Diego
on the hill of Tepeyac near Mexico City.

You left this beautiful portrait of yourself on his cloak.

May this book, like the portrait, be a sign and instrument
of your abiding presence with God's people.
From its pages speak to the hearts of my readers
as you spoke to all of us in your words to Juan Diego:
I will show and make known and give to mankind
all my love and my compassion,
my help and my protection.
I am your merciful Mother,
yours,
and all who are united in this land,
and all other peoples,
all who love me,
and call to me and seek me
and trust in me.

Introduction

Mary, the Mother of Jesus, is alive, and present with God's People. Her God and ours "is not a God of the dead, but of the living; for all live to him" (Luke 20:38). And all who live to him live to one another in him. For in the communion of the saints, all who are alive to God are in communion with one another, because they are in communion with the Lord.

Much of this book takes the form of prayerful conversation addressed to Mary. Conversation like this takes for granted Mary's communion with us in the Holy Spirit. In the course of the book we shall show the Scriptural justification for this belief in Mary's continuing presence with us and for our continuing conversation with her.

PART 1

the mother of jesus:

present with us

1

THE LISTENING MOTHER

Mary, you were always such a good listener! That's why you were such a good mother. You treasured in your heart all the words that were spoken about your child Jesus (Luke 2:19).

A mother has to be a good listener, one who hears and interprets every cry of her child. She knows in a flash whether the sound from the cradle is a cry of hunger, or simply a testing of vocal chords, a coo of contentment, or fascination with new-found lung power. Through the years a mother listens to every need of her child, whether he is an infant in the crib or a young man still trying to find himself, still searching for his identity.

In helping him find himself, a mother has to listen to what is crying out from her child's whole being. A child will listen willingly to his mother in obedience only if she has first listened to him, only if what she tells him to do corresponds to what he is already vaguely feeling in his very bones and flesh, and confusedly hearing in his heart and mind.

A mother can tell her child what is sounding in his own inner self, and can guide him accordingly, only because in attentive love she listens to all that is in him, and understands what he says by his actions even more clearly than what he says in his words. He will respond in ready obedience only to those words and directions which ring true to the authentic self which is already groping in him towards fulfillment. A mother educates by lovingly inviting forth what she finds already at work in the child.

Mary, you were a perfect listener. You pondered in your heart every word spoken concerning Jesus. You listened to every event in his life. You attended to every action in which he expressed what was in him. You heard every word in which he manifested his heart.

When you did not understand the words he spoke to you (Luke 2:50), you did not dismiss them with an indifferent shrug. Rather, you "kept all these things in your heart" (Luke 2:51), pondering them until you did understand. Love ever seeks understanding, and seeks till it finds. "When they did not find him, they returned to Jerusalem, seeking him" (Luke 2:45). Love finds understanding because it listens so attentively and searches so diligently.

Your listening heart detected the heart of God manifested in all that your Son said and did, for he himself is the Word of God, the revelation of God's love. Blessed are you who heard the word of God, not only from his lips, but speaking out in his whole person (Luke 11:27).

You listened to his whole being with your whole being. You were attentive to him with all your heart and soul, with all the fullness of your love. Is not that why you were able to say with such assurance at Cana, "Do whatever he tells you" (John 2:5)? You knew what he would do. For you had read far more in his heart than you had heard from his lips.

Learning from Your Son

You were always learning from your Son, just as every mother learns from her child. Is not this how every woman grows and becomes truly herself, truly a woman, through listening and responding in love, and maturing through this very listening and response? Every time Jesus spoke to you, you learned something new about him. Each question he asked you, each word he spoke to you, whether in his childhood or in the time of his public mission, caused you to revise your understanding of him.

Far from possessively moulding him into what you wanted him to be, you let him grow into what God wanted him to be, and you were ever in awe and wonderment at what was unfolding before you. Because you did not fully understand them, you pondered in your heart his words concerning his relationship with his heavenly Father: "Did you not know that I must be in my Father's house?" (Luke 2:49-50). For what was growing in him was greater than you could ever imagine, and you lovingly let it grow in God's way.

Thus, every mother must beware of moulding her child — God's child — according to her own narrow concepts of what he should be. Is not this the joy of growth of every true mother: to live in wondering amazement at the life which unfolds first in her womb, then in her arms, then before her eyes which follow her son wherever he goes.

All the child's unfolding is invited by the warmth of her love, by her cherishing appreciation of the limitless treasures of life which God has put into him and has entrusted to her.

Mother, did you not daily revise your ideas of what sort of child God had planted in your womb, and nourished at your breasts, and entrusted to your educating love? Did not God educate you through all that you saw unfolding in your Son?

How much you learned from watching your Son and listening to him! Only you can tell us what profound insights you had into his divine personality long before the light dawned for the rest of his disciples, long before these "riches of wisdom and knowledge" unfolded in the pondering heart of the Church in the course of the centuries (Colossians 2:3). Who, besides the Holy Spirit, is more capable than you of leading us into the infinite mystery of Jesus! Help us to see his glory!

Listen to Me, Mother

Mother, you were such a good listener to Jesus your Son when he was a child. Listen to me, who am also your son. We all need someone to listen to us as we express our hearts. No one can grow without a good listener, one whose listening heart understands. In speaking out our hearts in the presence of a loving attentive heart, we clarify ourselves to ourselves. Light comes to us when we open ourselves trustingly to a loving heart.

Mary, so much of our prayer to God takes this form. Just to know that he listens, even if we seem to hear nothing in response, enables us to open our hearts before him. And even if we never receive clear words from him, he does clearly respond to us in the light which comes to us as we speak ourselves out before him.

And this is not merely the natural enlightenment which comes in reflection. Since our reflection in prayer is really loving converse with God, his response comes in the form of inner light given to us by his Holy Spirit, revealing to us not only ourselves, but showing us his own loving heart. Thus, our persevering faith and our loving confidence in God are themselves an answer to our prayer. He has listened, and our confident faith itself is conviction that he has heard. My confidence in his love is often answer enough for me.

So it is in my relationship with you, Mother. Your very listening, even if you say not a word, is your answer to me. For what I need very much is such a listener, so that all that God has planted in me may grow.

I know from experience how God spoke to me in the love and concern of those who loved me: my father and mother, my brothers and sisters, my teachers, and my friends in the Lord. I know how the Spirit of God spoke in their love for me, in the corrections they gave me, and in the example they set me. That same Holy Spirit, dwelling in me just as he dwelt in them, caused my loving response to the love and concern for me which he inspired in them. I know that my earthly mother, though she is no longer in this world, still loves me and is still concerned about me. "Love remains forever" (1 Corinthians 13:8, 13).

Mary, your love is like that. I know that it is impossible for you, or for anyone else, to really love Jesus without loving also all those for whom he died. That is why I know that you love me and are concerned about me. I am "the brother for whom Christ died" (1 Corinthians 8:11), and therefore along with Christ I am your son. Therefore I know that you love me. And I know from experience that God's love in a human heart is always powerful to draw light and love from other hearts. God's love in your heart will draw love from my heart.

I have experienced your love for me, and your response to me, though not in the sense that I have ever heard your voice or seen your presence. Just as my faith in your Son is itself the infallable sign that he has spoken to me personally in my heart, so through the years my lasting confidence in you as my mother has been the sign and effect of your real maternal influence in my heart. Christians know the reality of your spiritual maternity precisely because they have experienced it.

Mother, I know that your listening heart is God's listening heart made exceedingly close to me. Did he not say through his prophet that his own heart has not only the characteristics of a father's heart, but all the characteristics of a mother's heart as well? "Can a woman forget her infant, be without tenderness for the child of her womb? Even should she forget, I will never forget you" (Isaiah 49:15).

What he said in these words of the prophet, he says more eloquently still in deeds, in revealing his heart to me in your heart, Mother Mary. Your loving heart impelled you to bring the Lord and his Spirit to the home of Elizabeth and Zechariah and their son John. Your compassionate heart turned to the embarrassed wedding couple at Cana, bringing them God's own love in the miracle of the water changed into wine.

Therefore as I reflect upon you in your presence, Mary, your listening heart will respond to me, you will speak to me through the Holy Spirit's interior light in my heart, and you will inflame my love for you, and for the Lord, your Son. Listen to my pondering heart!

2

MARY'S PONDERING HEART

"Blessed are those who hear the word of God and keep it" (Luke 11:29). Mary, St. Luke has described you as the perfect bearer and keeper of the word. He shows you listening to the word of God brought to you by Gabriel, pondering it carefully, wondering "what sort of greeting this might be" (Luke 1:29). You ask for clarification of the angel's message: "How can this be, since I do not know man?" (Luke 1:34). Then you act upon the word, surrendering yourself to it: "Behold, I am the Lord's servant; let it be done to me according to your word" (Luke 1:38).

Thus you consecrate yourself completely to the person and mission of your Son. And at once the Lord entrusts himself fully to you!

As God gradually brings his word to fulfillment in the deeds which he promised in his word, you ponder also these saving deeds of God, these events which he brings about in the power of his Spirit. These events are also a word from God, for God speaks to us in the deeds which he accomplishes according to his word.

That God speaks to us not only in words but also in events was brought out more accurately in the older translations of Luke's Gospel than in the contemporary versions. In a newer translation, for example, after the angel announces the Lord's birth to the shepherds, these say, "Let us go over to Bethlehem and see this **event** which the Lord has made known to us" (Luke 2:15,n). In an older translation, the shepherds say, "Let us go over to Bethlehem and see this **word** that is come to pass, which the Lord has shown to us" (Luke 2:15,d). It is true that a "word come to pass" is an "event." But it is an event spoken by the Lord, and therefore the event itself is a word of God.

In Hebrew thinking, an event brought about by God, especially when it was announced in advance, was considered a word of God, carrying profound meaning. Indeed, **dabar,** the Hebrew for **"word,"** also means "event." The Jewish people were keenly aware that God spoke to them in the salvation events which he brought about in their history.

The Greek word used by St. Luke, and translated either as "event" or "word," is **rhema** (plural, **rhemata).** **Rhema** occurs in several significant passages in which Luke tells us how you pondered God's word, Mary. For example, "Let us go over to Bethleham, and let us see this **word** that has come to pass, which the Lord has shown us. . . . And when they saw it, they made known the **word** that had been told them concerning this child. . . . But Mary kept all these **words,** pondering them in her heart" (Luke 2:15, 17, 19).

In this passage, the same Greek word **rhema** signifies both the **event** accomplished by God and the **word** in which he announced it to the shepherds. Mary, you ponder in your heart both the events and the words which announce and explain them. When **rhema** signifies **"event"** in Luke's writings, it could be translated "word-event," since God is speaking through the event, revealing his truth. A **rhema,** a word-event, is a "thing that has happened, which the Lord has made known" (Luke 2:15,r).

Again Luke writes, at the end of the story of the finding of the child Jesus in the temple, "They did not understand the saying **(rhema)** which he spoke to them. . . . His mother kept all these things (word-events, **rhemata)** in her heart" (Luke 2:50-51,r). Mary, no doubt Luke means that you pondered both the events and the words which Jesus spoke in the course of the events. For the events contained a divine mystery, a revelation from God. You continued to ponder the words and the word-events until you reached understanding of God's revelation. You are the perfect listener to God's word.

Thus, in Luke's story of your child's infancy we see God's way of revealing his truth. He gives his revelation through words and deeds, manifested to receptive, listening, pondering hearts. Luke presents you as the type of God's people, the Church, who are blessed in hearing God's word and keeping it (Luke 11:20).

When the shepherds at Bethlehem saw the word-event which God's word had announced to them, they in turn proclaimed what they had seen and heard (Luke 2:17). And your pondering heart penetrated ever more deeply into the mystery contained both in the words and in the word-events. All the word-events which you pondered were brought about by God in fulfillment of his word to you at the Annunciation. Therefore Elizabeth cries out to you, "Blessed is she who believed that there would be a fulfillment of what was spoken to her from the Lord" (Luke 1:45). We can only add, "Blessed are you whose faith continued to search ever more deeply into the meaning of these word-events, and to absorb the Lord's word completely!" For in due time, you shared with God's people your own more profound understanding of the mystery.

Mary's Role in Revelation

The whole believing Church owes an eternal debt of gratitude to your pondering heart, Mary. For you not only received into the world the Word of God, who is himself the fullness of revelation, you likewise received, in your faithful pondering of what God was doing in your life with Jesus, the Church's deepest understanding of the Word.

God can reveal his truth only to one who is open to receive it. Luke shows that you, in believing and pondering God's word, were perfectly open to his revelation. Believing is receiving. Pondering is a fullness of believing and receiving, for loving faith seeks to penetrate ever more profoundly into God's word. We can fully understand the Word only by experiencing the Word's work in our hearts, and by pondering what he is doing in us.

Mary, you were the first to receive all the fullness of God's saving Word and work into your heart, and you were the first to ponder this salvation thoroughly. You experienced God's revelation fully in your life, for in perfect faith you lovingly received the Word in person into your heart and into your womb, and he is the fullness of revelation. You pondered lovingly what he was accomplishing in you and in your life. You continued to ponder him and his work until it was finished. You were fully involved with him and his work, and thus you pondered in faith what you yourself were fully experiencing. Thus you gradually came to full understanding of the word.

Who can doubt that you know Jesus, the Word, as no one else does? Who better than you can lead us to Jesus and to a profound knowledge of him? You received the revelation of the Word through your very experience of him in your life, and you share this revelation and experience with us. For who but you revealed to Luke's heart the revelation which he shares with us in his chapters about the conception and infancy of your Son Jesus? Only one who has experienced Christ can lead others into this experience.

O Mary, be with us in the power of the Holy Spirit, as we ponder "the mystery that Christ is in us" (Colossians 1:27), the Christ who lived first in you! Help us to ponder your Son's saving presence in our hearts and in our lives, help us to come to a full realization of what he is doing in us, so that we can respond to his work with all our hearts, as you yourself responded to him when you said, "Behold the handmaid of the Lord! Be it done to me according to your word!"

You Are a Word

God's word is not simply the syllables strung together into the words and sentences of the Scriptures. God speaks to me in the persons as well as in the events presented to me in that written word. I must look at these persons and see what they do, and what God does in them, if I would understand the fullness of God's message to me. And his message is an invitation to become involved, like these persons, in these same saving events.

Therefore, Mary, I ponder everything that God's word tells me about you. I watch you in the events of your life with Jesus as described in the Scriptures. All that I see speaks to my heart. God speaks to me in the truth which comes alive for me in your person and action. You are a word from God to me. Your relationship with the Lord expresses the truth of what my relationship with him should be.

I watch you, for example, in the Annunciation scene.

I look at you in this word-event, and see your total response to God's word: "I am the Lord's servant; let it be done to me according to your word" (Luke 1:38).

You yourself have made the Annunciation scene alive for me, Mary, for your personal response to the word calls out to me as a word of love, inviting me to respond to the Lord in the way you did. Your gift of self to him invites me to make the total gift of myself to him. I cannot look at you in the Annunciation scene without saying spontaneously with all my heart, "I, too, am the Lord's servant; let it be done to me according to his word."

And I cannot hear your words of acceptance and self-giving at the Annunciation without thinking of Jesus in his agony and on the cross, saying, "Not my will, but thine be done!" Mother and Son think alike, and love alike.

This is what happens to me as I ponder the mysteries of Jesus while praying your Rosary, watching all the events of your life with Jesus your Son. Jesus was God's word to you and to me. He himself, and all the events of his life with you, speak to me as they spoke to you.

In watching your response to him in all the scenes in the gospels in which you and he are together, I am powerfully moved by the Holy Spirit to respond to him in the way that you did. This is because the purposes of God's love to which you responded are his purposes for me and for everyone.

When you responded to God, you responded not only for yourself, but also for me. By responding now in my own person, in the way that you did, I ratify what you did in responding for me. Only thus do I obtain the full benefit of your response.

The very power of your response to the Lord in the Spirit draws me to respond in the same Holy Spirit. Your generosity to the Lord still draws people like me to generosity like yours. O Mary, take all resistance from my heart! By your maternal love for me, and by your presence with me in the power of the Holy Spirit, help me to yield totally to the Lord!

I offer to God your own yielding to the Lord, as a prayer winning for me the grace to yield just as you did: "I am the Lord's servant. Let it be done to me according to your word!"

3

THE INFANT LORD

Mary, as I ponder with you the mysteries of your Son, the slain Lamb, I perceive that all the mysteries are but different facets of the one central Christian mystery: the mystery of Jesus Christ as Lord.

The Lord is God's Son and your Son. St. Paul provides us with a beautiful definition of Jesus as Lord: "God's Son, who was descended from David according to the flesh, and designated Son of God in power according to the Spirit of holiness by his resurrection from the dead: Jesus Christ our Lord" (Romans 1:4).

He was put to death in the human nature which he received from you as a descendant of David. By the power of God he was raised from death and constituted Son of God in power: the one who has the power to give the Holy Spirit to all.

"Lord" is a dynamic title, expressing dominion and the exercise of power. It signifies the life-giving power of the risen Son of God, his power to give life in the Spirit to all mankind. This title and power are given to him in the resurrection: "He humbled himself and became obedient unto death, even death on a cross; therefore God has highly exalted him and bestowed on him the name which is above every name, that at the name of Jesus . . . every tongue should confess that Jesus Christ is Lord" (Philippians 2:8-11).

Though strictly speaking his title "Lord" describes Jesus only as he is after his resurrection, St. Luke applies this title to him even while he is still in your womb, Mary. Luke reports for us Elizabeth's words to you at the Visitation: "Why is this granted to me, that the mother of my Lord should come to me!" (Luke 1:43). Likewise, the angel appearing to the shepherds at Bethlehem already gives Jesus this title which he will gain only in his resurrection: "To you is born this day in the city of David a Savior, who is Christ, the Lord" (Luke 1:11).

Everything that happens in any man's life is somehow forever after contained in that man. What St. Paul was at the end of his life, for example, was conditioned by all that he had done before and after his conversion. But thanks be to God, all that we have done, though it always remains in us, is marvelously transformed when we enter into the Lord's glory. The Lord's healing and life-giving power begins to work in us the moment we surrender to him in the fullness of faith, and gradually heals and recreates the totality of our life, till, like an immaculate virgin bride, we are ready for total union with the Lord, the divine Bridegroom. "For I betrothed you to Christ to present you as a pure bride to her one husband" (2 Corinthians 11:2).

So too the whole life of Jesus, even from his infancy in your womb, Mary, is somehow contained in him as risen Lord. For he redeemed the totality of human life by himself living a complete human life, from conception in your womb onwards to death on the cross and resurrection in glory. Therefore the totality of his life on earth is working through his saving power as risen Lord.

That is why St. Luke sees the Lord's whole earthly life from the point of view of his power and dominion as

Lord. His glorious lordship is the full perfection of his earthly life, and is in unbroken continuity with it. This is one of the key themes of Hebrews. As a true man, sharing fully in our human nature (Hebrews 2:12), like us in all things but sin (2:17; 4:15), Jesus grew to his full perfection as "Son of God in power" (Romans 1:4) through his loving obedience in sufferings (Hebrews 2:10). "Although he was a Son, he learned obedience through what he suffered, and being made perfect, he became the source of salvation to all who obey him" (Hebrews 5:8).

Therefore when we look at the mysteries of Jesus' earthly life as presented by St. Luke, we see them as already the Lord's mysteries, for through this life which he lived as one of us, he sanctifies us by his power as Lord. All the mysteries of his life are contained in him as risen Lord, and in his power in the Spirit, so that he can reproduce them in his people, in whom he continues to live his own life.

He carries on his redeeming work in us by reliving his complete life in each of his members, refashioning each one of us in the likeness of his own life, death and resurrection. All the mysteries of his infancy, childhood and hidden life, of his public life of preaching and healing, of his passion, death and resurrection, are to be reproduced and completed in his Body, the Church, and in each of his members in varying ways and degrees.

The Rosary

This truth is the theological basis for praying the Rosary. When we ponder with you the mysteries of your Son's life, Mary, while praying the Rosary, or reading the Scriptures, or gazing in loving faith on ikons, or other images showing the mysteries of his life, the Lord himself lives these mysteries in us, reproducing them in our hearts by his Spirit and power. While our lips are praying the Our Fathers and Hail Marys of the Rosary, our hearts are contemplating Jesus in his mysteries, drawing him into ourselves by our faith and love, so that he will relive his own life in us.

Here is how I ponder and enter into these mysteries as I pray the Rosary. My method involves three simple steps: Observe, Discern, Act.

1. *Observe*. I look at the word-event as it is described in the Scriptures. I am there, watching what is happening, listening to what is said. I am with the shepherds at Bethlehem, adoring the Infant who is Christ, the Lord. Or I am present with Thomas and the other apostles when the risen Lord suddenly appears in their midst and says, "Peace!"

2. Pondering, I *discern* how I am part of this mystery and how it has to be fulfilled in me. I must do what I see the people in the mystery doing. Their relationships with Jesus must be mine. Jesus says to me what he says to Thomas, "Do not be unbelieving, but believe!" (John 20:27).

3. I *act*. I do what the persons in the mysteries do. I do what Thomas does. I say, "My Lord and my God!" In this act of faith and adoration and self-giving to my Lord, I become involved with the Lord. I trust myself to him and he trusts himself to me.

1. I am present at the Annunciation. Mary, I listen as you say, "Behold the handmaid of the Lord! Be it done to me according to your word!"

2. I discern that if I trust myself to the Father in the way you did, Mary, the Holy Spirit will form Christ in me.

3. I act as you did, Mary, I offer my whole being to

my God. "I am your servant! Let the promises contained in your word be fulfilled in me!" And God entrusts his Son to me.

1. I am in the garden with Jesus, observing him in his agony, listening to his prayer, pondering his words to his disciples.

2. He says to me what he said to Peter and the other disciples, "Could you not watch one hour with me? Watch and pray, lest you enter into temptation."

3. I act; I watch and pray with Jesus. I pray as he did, "Father, not my will, but thine be done!"

1. I watch, Mary, as you are taken up, body and soul, into the full glory of the risen Lord, your Son, to share in his life-giving power as Lord; just as you shared in the totality of his obedience and suffering on earth.

2. I realize that he has shared his power in the Spirit with you, so that you can be my Mother, present with me in the Holy Spirit, so that you can form his life in me.

3. O Mary, assumed into heaven! Because in faith you pondered your Son's mysteries in your heart as you lived his life and his sufferings with him on earth, the totality of your earthly life with him has been caught up into his glory as risen Lord, and has been completely transformed by him. Thus in your glory you are the revelation of my hope for the same transformation. Heavenly Lady, be with me as I relive the Lord's mysteries in my heart while praying your Rosary. As I thus pray with you, fashion his life in me, just as you once fashioned him in your womb.

Obtain for me by your intercession that the Lord's redeeming power will transform gloriously not only the good that I have done, but will heal me of all the evil I have done. Clothe me for bridal union with the Lord in spotless holiness like your own. "The Spirit and the bride say, Come! And let each one who hears say, Come! Come, Lord Jesus!" (Revelation 22:17, 20).

In this way of praying the mysteries of Christ in using the Rosary, the Scriptures "come alive" for me. And Christ, "the word in its fullness" (Colossians 1:25), fills me with his own life, for I am open to him in a living relationship of faith, hope and love.

There are fifteen traditional mysteries of the Rosary.[1] But we are not limited to meditation on these when we pray the Rosary. Using the method just described, we may ponder any one of the word-events presented in the Scriptures. For example, we may join Peter in his great act of faith, "You are the Christ, the Son of the living God" (Matt. 16:16); or in his act of hope, "Lord, to whom shall we go? You have the words of eternal life" (John 6:68); or in his triple act of love, "Lord, you know everything. You know that I love you!" (John 21:17). Through such acts of faith, hope and love, we become deeply involved in the life of the Lord Jesus.

1. **The Five Joyful Mysteries**
    The Annunciation
    The Visitation
    The Nativity
    The Presentation
    The Finding of the Child Jesus

   The Five Sorrowful Mysteries
    The Agony of Jesus in the Garden
    The Scourging of Jesus
    The Crowning of Jesus with Thorns
    Jesus Carries His Cross
    Jesus Is Crucified

   The Five Glorious Mysteries
    The Resurrection
    The Ascension
    The Descent of the Holy Spirit
    Mary's Assumption into Heaven
    Mary's Coronation

Blessed Mary

O Mother, when we pray your Rosary, our heart ponders the mysteries of Jesus while our lips say the words of the Hail Mary. In this prayer, we declare you "Blessed among women." The word of God authorizes us to do this.

"As Jesus was speaking, a woman in the crowd raised her voice and said to him, 'Blessed is the womb that bore you, and the breasts that you sucked.' But he said, 'Blessed rather are those who hear the word of God and keep it'" (Luke 11:27-28).

This woman in the crowd calls you blessed because of your divine maternity. And in doing this she is completely in harmony with your own inspired words in the Magnificat: "Henceforth all generations will call me blessed, for he who is mighty has done great things for me, and holy is his name!" (Luke 1:48). By these "great things" you mean your motherhood of the Lord, for which Elizabeth has just called you blessed: "Blessed are you among women, and blessed is the fruit of your womb!" (Luke 1:42). Elizabeth is only the beginning of that long line of endless generations who call you "Blessed."

The woman in the crowd is completely in tune with you and with Elizabeth, who both spoke under the inspiration of the Holy Spirit. The Spirit himself inspired your grateful appreciation of God's mighty work in making you Mother of the Lord. The woman, too, calls you blessed because you are the Mother of God.

At first sight, the response of Jesus to the woman in the crowd seems to deny that this is why you are blessed. Blessedness, he says, consists rather in receiving God's word and in being faithful to it.

In reality, Jesus is not denying that you are blessed

because you are his mother. Were he denying this, he would be denying the truth. He is calling attention to another aspect of your blessedness, one in which we must all share. Certainly if anyone has been faithful in hearing and keeping God's word, it has been you, Mary! St. Luke presents you as the perfect model for all who hear and keep the word. It was precisely your faithfulness to the word that opened you to receive the Word of God in person into your womb.

Therefore to say that you are blessed in hearing the word of God and keeping it is not to deny that you are blessed also, and above all, in bearing the Word of God lovingly in your womb. Elizabeth, filled with the Holy Spirit, declared you blessed in both ways: "Blessed is she who believed that there would be a fulfillment of what was spoken to her from the Lord!" (Luke 1:45), and, "Blessed are you among women, and blessed is the fruit of your womb!" (Luke 1:42).

Thus Elizabeth set the pattern for the fulfillment of your own prophetic words in which you declared, "Henceforth all generations will call me blessed" (Luke 1:48).

The Scriptures, then, fully authorize us to call you "Blessed," and to address you in the Scriptural words of the Hail Mary: "Rejoice, Mary, full of grace, the Lord is with you. . . . Blessed are you among women, and blessed is the fruit of your womb, Jesus!" (Luke 1:28,45).

The rest of the Hail Mary is scripturally accurate as well. For Jesus praises the tax collector who said, "O God, be merciful to me, a sinner" (Luke 18:13). The consciousness of my sinfulness does not shake my hope, for God has been born of a woman, and thus has become like me in all things but sin. And when he was dying for me, a sinner, Jesus commended me to you, his mother, saying, "Behold your mother!" (John 19:27). The Mother of God is my mother!

Mother, till the hour when I die with Jesus, I will still be a sinner in process of being redeemed. Till then I shall continue to trust in your maternal support and intercession, and shall always pray, "Holy Mary, Mother of God, pray for us sinners, now, and at the hour of our death."

4

THE TEMPLE OF GLORY

O Mary, in the Annunciation scene St. Luke presents you to us as the temple in which the Glory of the Lord is present and manifest.

"The Glory of the Lord" in the Old Testament was a manifestation of God's presence and power. Usually it was a brilliant light or fire expressing the inaccessible majesty of God, which was nonetheless present among men. It was often veiled in a cloud by which its brilliance was tempered and filtered through. On the day when Solomon's temple was dedicated, "a cloud filled the house of the Lord, so that the priests could not stand to minister because of the cloud; for the glory of the Lord filled the house of the Lord" (1 Kings 8:10).

This was a repetition of what had happened when Moses set up the tabernacle for God in the desert. The tabernacle was God's tent in the midst of his people, who also dwelt in tents. When Moses had finished the work of preparing the tabernacle, "the cloud *overshadowed* the tent of meeting, and the glory of the Lord filled the tabernacle" (Exodus 40:34).

Mary, these words of Exodus are clearly echoed by Gabriel's words to you at the Annunciation: "The Holy Spirit will come upon you, and the power of the Most High will *overshadow* you; therefore the child to be born will be called holy, the Son of God" (Luke 1:35).

When the power of the Most High overshadows you,

Mary, you become the tabernacle filled with the Lord's Glory, for God's Son now dwells in your womb. In you and your Son, the inaccessible holiness of God is brought close to us and becomes fully accessible. It is filtered through to us, as it were, so that we are not blinded and destroyed by its brilliance.

Not only during the time when God was an infant in your womb, or a child in your arms, were you the temple of God's Glory. Through your loving contact with the living God, your Son, your whole person was forever afterwards transformed by his holiness; for he dwelt in your heart through faith in a more blessed way than in your womb. In your person was verified first and most perfectly what St. Paul says about all true believers: "We all, with unveiled face, beholding the Lord's glory, are being changed into his likeness from one degree of glory to another" (2 Corinthians 3:18).

After Moses spoke face to face with God on Mount Sinai, God's glory shone on his face, and the people were afraid to come near him (Exodus 34:29). Therefore Moses "put a veil over his face so that the Israelites might not see the end of the fading splendor" (2 Corinthians 3:13). When a man turns to the Lord Jesus in faith, says Paul (2 Corinthians 3:16), the veil of unbelief is removed from his heart, and he gazes on "the glory of God in the face of Christ" (2 Corinthians 4:6). He sees that Jesus is "the Glory," the presence and manifestation of God.

"And we all, with unveiled face, beholding the glory of the Lord, are being changed into his likeness from one degree of glory to another; for this comes from the Lord, who is the Spirit" (2 Corinthians 3:18). That is, when we contemplate the Lord Jesus in Christian faith, his Holy Spirit works in us, transforming us into the Lord's glory, filling us with his divine life and holiness. "Look to him and be radiant" (Psalm 34:5).

Mary, you were incessantly contemplating the Lord Jesus in faith, for you were always pondering in your heart everything concerning him. You lived in faith, "with face unveiled," receiving ever-increasing enlightenment from the Spirit of God. The overshadowing Spirit had not only formed the Lord Jesus in your womb, but he transformed your person into the Lord's likeness, from one degree of glory to another, as you contemplated your Son in faith. You daily grew in holiness and glory through your incessant contact with him. How totally transformed with divine glory and holiness you came to be, you lived thirty years in the immediate presence of the Lord of Glory!

What is true of you in a unique degree is to be accomplished in all Christian believers, in proportion to their openness to Jesus in faith and love and prayer. That is why St. Luke presents you not just as the temple of the Glory, but as the type of the whole people of God. They, with you, are to be filled with the glory of the divine presence.

Drawn by Your Holiness

When Moses saw the Glory of God burning in the bush, he was powerfully drawn to it. That is a characteristic of God's holiness whenever it is manifested. Though it fills the beholder with a profound awe and religious dread, at the same time it has a loving attractiveness about it which gently invites the beholder. "I must go and look at this strange sight and see why the bush is not burnt" (Exodus 3:3).

Just as Moses was drawn to the burning bush, so we are drawn to God's glory dwelling in you, Mother of Jesus!

Christians are drawn to you first of all not because they have requests to make of you. They are attracted to you primarily because God's presence and holiness in you draws them. Recognizing this fact, the Church for centuries has compared you to the burning bush: "The indestructible burning bush seen by Moses signifies for us your praiseworthy and never-destroyed virginity; O Mother of God, pray for us!" (Liturgy for the Feast of Mary's Maternity, January 1).

Filled with God's presence and holiness, Mary, you are a manifestation of the Lord God among us. You are "the woman clothed with the sun" (Revelation 12:1), the Lady of Light. This is true of you before it becomes true of the rest of the Church. The holiness of God radiates from you in a spiritual luminosity. The aura of God surrounds you and draws us to him who is manifest in you.

Mary, this is how your influence has always been experienced in Christian life. We come to you drawn by the God who is present and manifest in you. We come to you in the desire of sharing in your own intimate communion with the Holy God. And you are powerful in bringing us into this communion, for you are filled with the Holy Spirit of the Lord. You are one of our great aids to prayer. You are a living sacrament of the divine presence. We cannot look at you in the Annunciation, praying in complete openness to the glory of the Lord, without being drawn by the Spirit into your own attitude of openness and expectation.

Your virginity is essentially a spiritual quality. It is your wholehearted faith seeking the Lord alone in purity of heart. In purity of heart you were ever open to the Lord to be filled with his glory. Your whole being cries out to us, "Look to the Lord and be radiant!" (Psalm 34:5).

God's People Is the Temple

Mary, as temple of the Glory, drawing all who see you to the holiness of God, you are type of the virgin Church. For God's whole people is the temple of God, transformed in faith by the Lord's glory, and drawing all nations to this holiness, that they too may be transformed. The whole people of God, says Zephaniah, will be the dwelling place of God in the eschatological days: "Rejoice, exult with all your heart, daughter Jerusalem. . . . The Lord, the King of Israel is in your midst" (Zephaniah 3:14). Gabriel echoes these words when he says to you, "Rejoice, full of grace, the Lord is with you!" (Luke 1:28).

In your person, as true Daughter of Jerusalem and Temple of God's Glory, Zephaniah's prophecy has its initial fulfillment. The Book of Revelation shows its broader fulfillment in the Church of the risen Lord: "I saw a new Jerusalem, the holy city, coming down out of heaven from God, beautiful as a bride prepared to meet her husband. . . . 'This is God's dwelling among men . . .' The city had no need of sun or moon, for the glory of God gave it light, and its lamp was the Lamb. The nations shall walk by its light" (Revelation 21:2-3; 22:23).

This vision of Revelation is fulfilled first of all in your person, Mary, in your coronation as Queen of Heaven. The mystery of your coronation is thus pledge and promise of the same fulfillment for all the people of God. Your Annunciation and your coronation are somehow one and the same mystery, at its initial and final stages of fulfillment, and we are invited into this mystery that it may be fulfilled in us.

O Mary at the Annunciation! When I look at you overshadowed by the power of God and receiving the Holy Spirit, and filled with the glory of the only Son of

God, I too am eager to be a temple of his glory, with you and all his people! Queen of Heaven, crowned with glory and honor, help me into that glory!

Come, Lord Jesus, fill me with your presence and glory!

5

WITH CHILD OF THE HOLY SPIRIT

"Now the birth of Jesus Christ took place in this way. When his mother Mary had been betrothed to Joseph, before they came together, she was found to be with child of the Holy Spirit" (Matt. 1:18,r). The evangelist does not say simply, "she was found to be with child." He adds, "of the Holy Spirit."

Who first discovered that you were with child, Mary? You yourself, of course. You experienced in your womb the reality of the child who was growing there: "She found that she was with child by the Holy Spirit" (Matt. 1:18,e). Thus was verified the truth which you had already believed on God's word:

"The Holy Spirit will come upon you and the power of the Most High will overshadow you" (Luke 1:35).

"Blessed is she who believed that there would be a fulfillment of what was spoken to her from the Lord!" (Luke 1:45). Mary, you experience that fulfillment in your womb, and you are blessed with the presence of the child whom you have received directly from God in faith. Believing is receiving. You are blessed in receiving God's son as your own Son. You are the blessed Mother of God, the blessed Virgin!

When you first believed the Lord's word telling you that you would conceive by the Holy Spirit, you responded at once in love, and expressed your faith by making the total gift of yourself to the Lord: "Behold, I am the hand-

31

maid of the Lord: let it be done to me according to your word" (Luke 1:38). Thus you consecrated yourself to the Person and mission of your Son.

Later, when you experienced the living reality of the child in your womb, you expressed your faith anew in your heart: "My child is there by the power of the Holy Spirit!" And you renewed and deepened your consecration of yourself to your Son. What a blessed experience it was for you each time you felt the stir of that child in your womb! Each time you must have expressed once again your faith in God's word that the child was there by the power of the Holy Spirit!

When you began to experience the child in your womb, certainly you must have told Joseph, your fiancé, about it. Since you were betrothed to him, this matter intimately concerned him. A child in the womb of a wife-to-be is certainly of concern to her husband-to-be! In your love for Joseph and in loyalty to your betrothal to him, you wanted to explain the whole matter to him, unbelievable though it seemed to be.

Could you expect him to believe it? You knew that Joseph was a man of profound faith. The evangelist tells us that he was a just man (Matt. 1:19). This is equivalent to saying that he was a man of faith, like Father Abraham. Abraham believed the Lord, and his faith was credited to him as justice (Gen. 15:6; Rom 4:22). A just man is a man who is subject to God in faith, and acts only in that faith and in accordance with it.

Mary, because you knew that Joseph was a just man, you could risk telling him about this divine mystery. You could trust that he would believe God's word about it when you relayed it to him. You told him the message you had received from Gabriel, and he accepted it in faith. He believed not only because of your witness to it, your testimony that you were experiencing its verification in your womb, but also because at the same time he was moved interiorly to this faith by the Holy Spirit.

"Her husband Joseph, being a just man and unwilling to put her to shame, resolved to divorce her quietly" (Matt. 1:19,r). Many readers of these words suppose that Joseph must have thought that you were a victim of seduction and had conceived your child by another man, and therefore he wanted to put you away. But in reality, it was precisely because he believed that your child was of the Holy Spirit that Joseph was thinking of stepping out of your life. Because he was a just man and did not wish to bring this matter out into the open, he was thinking of divorcing you without publicity. People would not understand the divine mystery which prompted the divorce, and, as a just man, Joseph wanted to spare you from gossip.

But why divorce you if he knew there was no guilt whatsoever in your pregnancy, and believed that your child was of the Holy Spirit?

Because he dared not enter into this divine mystery uninvited. He was filled with such reverential awe in the presence of this divine mystery that he feared to stay. He wanted to depart from you quietly. Like Moses, he was impelled to "take off his shoes" (Compare Exodus 3:15), and withdraw in humility from the presence of the fiery holiness of God. One does not enter the presence of the Holy One uninvited. "When I summon him, he shall approach me; how else should one take the deadly risk of approaching me? says the Lord" (Jer. 30:21,n).

Joseph's humble fear to enter in where angels dare not tread is implied in the angel's words to him, "Joseph, son of David, **do not fear** to take Mary your wife, for that which is conceived in her is of the Holy Spirit" (Matt. 1:20). In referring to the conception by the Holy Spirit, the angel is not telling Joseph something he did not al-ready know from you, Mary, but is telling him not to be afraid of what he knows. It is because he knows that your child is of the Holy Spirit that he fears to take you home as his wife. He fears to live unbidden in the presence of this divine mystery of holiness.

But the angel of the Lord calls him into the holiness, telling him not to be afraid. Yes, that which is in her is of the Holy Spirit, but do not fear to take your wife and the holy Presence which consecrates her. The fact that her child is of the Holy Spirit should not make you withdraw in fear, for God calls you into this mystery to play a part in it. You have a mission in regard to Mary and her Son. You are to accept him as your own Son, and exercise your paternal authority by giving him his name: "She will bear a son, and you shall call his name Jesus, for he will save his people from their sins" (Matt. 1:21).

For how can this child, conceived virginally of the Holy Spirit, be Son of David if he does not have a human father of David's line? Joseph, son of David, in receiving your wife and accepting her Son as your own, you are making him, too, Son of David.

In telling us of these events, St. Mattew accepts the truth of the virginal conception of Jesus. He shows how even though Jesus is conceived of the Holy Spirit without a human father, he is nevertheless Son of David, because Joseph, son of David, accepts him as his own Son. Called by God, Joseph lives in the midst of the divine holiness, and Jesus, his adopted Son, lives in the family of David. "When Joseph woke from sleep, he did as the angel of the Lord commanded him; he took his wife, but knew her not until she had borne a son; and he called his name Jesus" (Matt. 1:24-25).

6

THE REVELATION OF MARY'S VIRGINITY

When Luke writes, "Mary kept all these words, pondering them in her heart" (Luke 1:19), he implies, Mother, that you yourself are the source from whom we have learned the mysteries which he is relaying to us.

Who but you, Mary, could have told us about your virginal conception of Jesus by the power of the Holy Spirit? This divine reality is a truth which we can know only by God's revelation. But God revealed this truth first of all to you.

No doubt in the years after the Lord's resurrection you confided this truth to your intimate friends, and especially to St. John, whom Jesus had entrusted to you as a son when he was dying on the cross. Was not John given to you as a son so that you might be his mother and teacher? You were to teach him many aspects of the mystery of Jesus which only you could know. And in teaching him, you were teaching us, for John, as our representative, received all these truths from you for us.

Since the virginal conception was a truth which the whole people of God needed to know, John passed this truth on to the community of believers, and to St. Luke. Or did you yourself tell it directly to Luke? Luke must have known you personally and intimately, since he writes about you so beautifully and lovingly.

You told of the marvels the Lord had done in you,

his humble handmaid. "He who is mighty has done great things for me; holy is his name!" (Luke 1:48). It was in the very doing of these great things for you, Mother, that God revealed this truth for us. The "words" which you kept, pondering them in your heart, were God's deeds in you, through which he spoke his truth. He revealed the virginal conception to you in your very experience of it and in his word in advance explaining that experience. You alone directly experienced this work of God in your womb, and so you alone could tell it to us. You pondered it deeply in the light of God's word which had announced it to you beforehand.

With what delicacy you must have spoken when you confided to John and to Luke, not only the mystery of the virginal conception of Jesus, but also the mystery of your consequent perpetual virginity. These friends, in turn, passed the revelation on to us with the same kind of delicacy. For these are truths which we all need to know, since they are an inseparable part of the mystery of the incarnation and of our virginal rebirth into the new creation.

St. Luke delicately tells us of your perpetual virginity by recording for us your brief words to the angel, "How can this be, since I do not know man?" (Luke 1:34).

"I Do Not Know Man"

Mary, when you found yourself with child of the Holy Spirit in fulfillment of God's word, and reflected on the meaning of this, you began to realize the tremendous consequences this would have in your life. One of these consequences was perpetual virginity. For when you experienced the reality of Jesus living in your womb, you renewed and deepened the total consecration of yourself

to him which you had made at the Annunciation. Thenceforth your whole heart and soul and mind and strength
were centered completely upon Jesus and his God-given
work, and you could live only for him and his mission.
Thus you committed yourself to perpetual virginity for
the kingdom. From then on you could beautifully express
the fact of your perpetual virginity in the words, "I do
not know man." Luke could highlight your virginal conception of Jesus by showing you to us, speaking these
words to the angel (Luke 1:34).

The same sort of things can be said of Joseph, your
husband. As he too reflected, with you, upon the Son
formed in your womb by the Spirit of God, and upon his
own God-given commission to accept this Son as his own,
he too lovingly focused the totality of his person upon this
Son and his mission, and, with you, committed himself to
perpetual virginity. Thus Joseph's own perpetual virginity
in his marriage with you was not only a consequence of
his profound reverence for you as virgin mother, it was a
consequence also of his total focusing of his life, with you,
upon Jesus and his work. Mary, you and your husband
Joseph were the first to practice virginity for the kingdom
(Matt. 19:12).

Virginity for the Kingdom

When it is authentically "for the kingdom" (Matt.
19:12), virginity or celibacy is experienced as a grace of
total concentration of one's whole person upon the Person
of the Lord in whom the kingdom comes. It is loving
availability to him and his mission in establishing that
kingdom, in complete freedom from all which would
impede this availability. The celibate is so "captivated"
(Philippians 3:12) by the Lord that he lives only for him
in complete consecration. In this total captivation by the

Lord, he is psychologically incapable of giving himself totally to any other person, as long as he remains faithful to his concentration upon the Lord.

Mary and Joseph, your virginal marriage was psychologically possible because both of you were so completely focused upon the Lord that you were absorbed in him and consumed in him, and so could live a virginal marriage, loving and serving each other only in Jesus. Your virginal concentration on Jesus did not interfere with your true love for each other, but deepened it.

In this one delicate phrase, "I do not know man," Luke reveals to us, Mary, all that you had confided to your friends about the virginal conception and about the perpetual virginity consequent upon it. You had accepted this perpetual virginity lovingly as part of your total consecration to Jesus and your complete concentration upon him and his work.

This work of God in you, this grace of perpetual virginity expressing your total consecration to Jesus, was something which grew in you. It was a further development of your self-giving to the Lord at the Annunciation in accepting virginal maternity. But Luke, looking at all this from the vantage point of its full development in the later years when you revealed it to your friends, sums it all up for us in those simple words, "How can this be, since I do not know man?" Receiving from the Christian community the divinely revealed truth about your perpetual virginity, Luke records this truth in those few words, "I do not know man."

Virgin Before, In, and After

Whatever the details in the process in which God revealed to us the truth about your perpetual virginity, the believing Church has always accepted this truth as divinely revealed, and has proclaimed it as a doctrine of Christian faith: Mary is a virgin before, in, and after the conception and birth of Jesus.

Not only the Roman Church, but the Eastern Orthodox Churches have always professed their faith in this truth of your abiding virginity. In their ikons picturing you, there are always three stars on your veil, symbolizing that you are virgin before, in, and after your Son's conception and birth.

Though there is disagreement these days about the meaning of the Scriptures concerning your virginity, it must be remembered that God did not give us the Scriptures in order to cause confusion. God speaks in order to be understood, and he gave his Church the gift of being able to understand and interpret his word. "He opened their minds to understand the Scriptures. . . . Beginning with Moses and all the prophets, he interpreted to them in all the Scriptures the things concerning himself" (Luke 24:45,27). By the light of the Holy Spirit, the risen Lord leads his Church into all the truth. "When the Spirit of truth comes, he will guide you into all the truth" (John 16:13).

It is to be expected, then, that the believing Church has a gift of believing and interpreting and proclaiming the full truth about your virginity, Mary. Any explanations which we give of the Scriptures must be carefully checked against what the believing Church has proclaimed through the centuries on the point in question. Likewise, the Church's proclamations of the truth must always be in accord with the Scriptures.

The Church has always explained your virginity as historical reality, and not as a mere myth concocted by the Church to express other divine truths. In his story of your conception of Jesus, Luke is already interpreting for us some of the divine truths implied and expressed in the historical facts which God worked in you. Luke's words "proclaim the works of God and clarify the mystery contained in them" (Vatican II, DV 2). The truth of your virginal conception and perpetual virginity are intimately connected with the whole mystery of Jesus. We can rightly and fully appreciate the mystery of Jesus only with the help of this truth about your virginity.

Your virginal conception of Jesus is not a myth to express meaning, but is a fact wrought by God to express meaning. God teaches by what he does and by the way in which he does it. In forming his Son in your womb in a virginal way by the power of the Holy Spirit, he conveyed profound meaning to us concerning the reality of our own virginal birth into God by the power of the Spirit of the Son. Let us look into this more closely.

7

MOTHER OF GOD

When the time had fully come
God sent forth his Son
born of woman . . .
so that we might receive adoption as sons.
And because we are sons,
God has sent the Spirit of his Son into our
    hearts
crying, "Abba, Father!" (Galatians 4:4-6).

O heavenly Father, these words of your apostle Paul tell me about the Mother of Jesus than any other passage of the Scriptures. They tell me that she is Mother of God, and they tell me why you have made her Mother of God. You did this so that I, too, like your Son, might be born of God. "The mere name **Theotokos,** Mother of God, contains the whole mystery of the economy of salvation."[1]

Father, to receive the Spirit of your Son is to be adopted into your Son. It is to be empowered to live in the Holy Spirit of love, in your Son's own filial relationship with you, his Father. Thus, through the same Holy Spirit who formed your Son in Mary's womb, we are born into your Son's own eternal birth in your bosom, so that with him we can truly call you Father. To be adopted as your sons and daughters in the Son, is to be born into the very life of the Holy Trinity!

---

[1]St. John Damascene, **De Fide Orth., 3:12.**

41

The Virgin Birth and Our Birth into God

> The Holy Spirit will come upon you,
> and the power of the Most High will over-
> shadow you;
> and for that reason the holy child to be born
> will be called "Son of God" (Luke 1:35).

O Mother Mary, since the person you conceive and bring forth is Son of God, God alone is his Father, and you are his virgin mother. Your Son has no earthly father. You conceive him by the power of the Holy Spirit. He is forever "the only Son who is in the bosom of the Father" (John 1:18). You receive him directly from the Father's eternal bosom! Thus your virginity is inseparable from your maternity. As Mother of God, you are virgin Mother.

We profess in the Creed that even in his humanity Jesus your Son is "God from God, light from light, true God from true God, begotten, not made, one in being with the Father." You conceive him because God's own love is poured out into your heart and into your womb by the Holy Spirit who is given to you.

It seems that John the Evangelist was very conscious of your virginal maternity when he wrote of Jesus, "To all who received him, who believed in his name, he gave power to become children of God; who were born, not of blood, nor of the will of the flesh, nor of the will of man, but *of God*" (John 1:12-13). For we can be born of God only virginally, and only in the Son of God born of a virgin.

It is even possible that in this verse John was speaking directly of your virginal maternity, Mary. For there is ancient manuscript evidence which seems to indicate that John wrote in the singular, referring to Jesus, "who *was* born not of blood, nor of the will of the flesh, nor of the will of man, but of God" (John 1:13, Jerusalem Bible). Other manuscript evidence, however, seems to indicate that John wrote in the plural and was referring to believers in Jesus. "Who *were* born not of blood . . . but of God."

Whichever John wrote, either reading expresses the same truth: Because Jesus was born virginally of a woman by the power of the Holy Spirit, we can be born virginally of God in that same Holy Spirit.

Thus your virginity is significant, Mary, not only for the uncreated Person who has no earthly father, Jesus, "begotten, not made." It is significant for us, too, for our birth into God through your Son can be only virginal. In your Son's birth from your womb by the power of the Holy Spirit, I am born into his eternal birth by the power of the same Spirit! Could I ever have believed that I have power to be born of God, if the Son of God had not been born of a virgin!

Mary, all this is what your virginal motherhood means to me.

When I see you overshadowed by the power of the Holy Spirit at the Annunciation, or pregnant with the Son of God in the Visitation, there leaps forth spontaneously from my heart a desire in faith and hope to be born into your Son's eternal birth in the bosom of the Father, by the power of the same Holy Spirit who formed this Son in your virginal womb.

Mary, your own perfect love for God, and your faith in his word, drew down this Spirit into your heart and womb. Mother, protect and nourish me in the womb of your love until I see the light of that eternal day when I will be born into the fullness of your Son's glory with the Father.

New Creation in Mary's Virginity

St. Irenaeus wrote, "The same Word of God who had raised up the first Adam from the virgin earth, came in the fullness of time to raise up this other Adam in the womb of a virgin" (MG 7:954-56). Irenaeus thus helps us to penetrate the full meaning of your virginal conceiving of Jesus. It is like a new creation of man raised up in the race of Adam by God's power.

Mary, your virginity is the beginning of the new creation. Our God told us in the Old Testament that he would revivify all things by his Spirit, and would create a new people, and renew the face of the earth. He begins this work in you, forming the new Adam in your womb in virginal conception. The fact that Jesus was born of a woman by the power of the Holy Spirit is the very expression of this radical re-creation.

In Christian faith we believe that we are in a world in which God intervenes, and that there are things that he alone is able to do. Love does such things. What right have we to limit this sovereign liberty of love by doubts about your virginal motherhood, Mary?

O Virgin Mary, in honoring your virginity and accepting its reality, I am professing faith in a fundamental way. I am proclaiming that my salvation and life in God come not from within the power of this created universe, but solely from God. The Apostle says to all of us, "By his grace you have been saved through faith; and this is not your doing, it is the gift of God" (Ephesians 2:8). All birth to life in God is virginal. It is not of flesh and blood, it can only be of the Spirit of God, given by Christ as pure gift.

Born to Shed His Blood

Thus, I see, O Virgin Mary, how crucial your virginal maternity is in the whole economy of salvation. Of a virgin mother God was born! If God was not born, if your Son is not God, then God did not die for me, and I cannot be born of God! If your Son is not God, if you did not give him flesh and blood, then he had no flesh to be crucified for me, no blood to shed for me, and I cannot be born of God!

But God did die for me. It was not simply a good man who died for me. God's Son died for me. God did not merely take on the appearance of man, he did not just pretend to be man, he truly became man. "The Word became flesh" (John 1:14), and as flesh he lived among us, as flesh he died for us. And he rose again from death to take us into the very glory of God, to transform us in this glory.

O Mother of God, since you gave your Son the flesh which was nailed to the cross, you are an integral part of the paschal mystery. God's blood shed for us is your blood! Thank you, Mother! How closely bound up with your virginal motherhood is the whole Christian mystery of the death and resurrection of Jesus, and of our virginal birth into God by the power of this death and resurrection!

How right John Damascene was when he said, "The mere name **Theotokos,** Mother of God, contains the whole mystery of the economy of salvation." Belief that you are virgin Mother of God is essential to belief in our own rebirth into God's own life. That is why your virginal conception of Jesus is explicitly professed in the Nicene Creed: "conceived by the Holy Spirit, born of the virgin Mary, suffered under Pontius Pilate. . . ."

Mary, when I address you as "Mother of God," in a sense I am saying everything that can be said of you. I proclaim in this title all that you are for Jesus, all that you are for God, all that you are for me, and for all God's children. To be mother of God is your fundamental prerogative, and the basis for all else that you are for God and for us.

8

MARY'S VIRGINITY AND
HER LOVE FOR JOSEPH

Mary, your virginal conjugal love for your husband Joseph, and his reciprocal love for you, merged together as one love. And this one love was a source from which love flowed far and wide, reaching all mankind, embracing all into your holy family.

Though you conceived your Son by the overshadowing power of God, Joseph is nonetheless your husband. "Joseph, son of David, do not fear to take Mary *your wife,* for that which is conceived in her is of the Holy Spirit" (Matthew 1:20). The divine command to Joseph to take you home included God's will that Joseph love and cherish you as his wife. Your mutual love certainly included all that is deepest and most lasting in conjugal love, even if there was no expression of this love in sexual union.

Your virginal conception of Jesus by the power of the Holy Spirit was in no way a denial of the dignity and beauty of the sexual union in which other wives and husbands express their conjugal love. For your virginity in maternity points up the true dignity of Christian marriage and sexual union. It shows that every child begotten of man and woman is destined to be born again in Christ as child of God. What good is it to be born into this world if that is all there is to life! "If for this life only we have hoped in Christ, we are of all men most to be pitied!" (1 Corinthians 15:19). It is precisely for resurrection in Jesus into God's own glorious life that we were born into this world and redeemed by the blood of Jesus.

Nor did your virginal conception of Jesus lessen or harm the conjugal love existing between you and Joseph. Rather, your virginal relationship with Joseph helps us to understand the best elements in all conjugal love.

Your virginal love for Joseph, far from being a denial of the dignity of the love expressed in sexual union, is a witness to what is most authentic and permanent in conjugal love, namely, the self-sacrificing love in which husband and wife love each other as "the brother and sister for whom Christ died" (1 Corinthians 8:12). This is the element of conjugal love which the New Testament highlights most. "Husbands, love your wives as Christ loved the Church and gave himself up for her" (Ephesians 5:25).

Christ's own self-sacrificing love is poured out into the hearts of Christian spouses, and transforms and ennobles all the other elements of their love. The Lord's love in their hearts takes into itself and transforms all that is good and beautiful in their human love, their family love, and their sexual love. In their sexual union, as in every other element of their relationship, husband and wife are to love each other with Christ's own transcending love, in which he gave his life "that he might present the Church to himself in splendor" as his bride (Ephesians 5:27), so that all those for whom he died might be united with him in bridal union.

When consecrated virgins and other Christian celibates, true to their vocation, love their fellowmen in Christ, they love with this transcending love, this love

which breaks through all the limitations of flesh and blood
relationship, and loves every person precisely as "the
brother for whom Christ died" (1 Corinthians 8:12).
Mary, in love like this, your own maternal love for your
Son Jesus broke all the natural limits of your love for
him as your flesh and blood, and reached out to embrace
all those who became his brothers and sisters through faith
in him as crucified Lord.

Your virginal motherhood of the sisters and brothers
for whom Christ died is thus the prototype of all virginal
love in the Church. The consecrated virgin and the Christian celibate are called by Jesus to witness to this kind of
love, a love which transcends the natural limits of the
home, of family love, of conjugal love, of racial love, and
reaches out to love everyone with the same love with
which Christ loved the whole Church and delivered himself up for her. "For in Christ Jesus you are all sons of
God through faith. For as many of you as were baptized
into Christ have put on Christ. There is neither Jew nor
Greek, there is neither male nor female (nor husband and
wife, nor parent and child), for you are all one in Christ
Jesus" (Galatians 3:26-28).

Mary, your love embraced all mankind. It broke out
of the limits of the tiny home at Nazareth, and accepted
all of us as your sons and daughters. Celibacy witnesses
to unrestricted love like this. Since celibacy for the kingdom is such a striking witness to this transcending element
in Christian love, it is witness also to what is most precious
and lasting in Christian conjugal love: the spouses' love
for each other as brother and sister for whom Christ died,
destined for the most intimate union with him, the divine
Bridegroom.

Thus, Christian celibate abstention from marriage
and sexual union is in no way intended as a despising of

sex and marriage, but is rather a witness of what is most beautiful in all human relationships: love for one another as persons called to an intimate bridal union with the Lord Jesus himself, the Bridegroom of each and of all.

Mary's Absorption in Jesus

Mary, we have spoken of your perpetual virginity in terms of your total concentration upon Jesus and consecration to him. This complete absorption in your Son, the Word, is manifest in the way you incessantly pondered all the word-events concerning him.

Luke draws a contrast between your response and the response of others who heard and saw these words and works of God. After the birth of John the Baptist, "all these things (the word-events concerning John) were talked about through all the hill country of Judea" (Luke 1:65). Elizabeth's relatives and friends spread the good news everywhere! Likewise the shepherds who had heard God's word from the angel, and saw what this word announced, "made known the word which had been told them concerning this child. . . . But Mary kept all these word-events and pondered them in her heart" (Luke 2:17-19).

Mary, in quiet contrast to the shepherds and friends of Elizabeth, who symbolize the preachers of the word, you become completely absorbed in loving contemplation of the mystery revealed in the words and works; and that mystery is the Person Jesus. You become totally absorbed in Jesus, and in all that he is for us.

We must be listeners and ponderers of the word if in turn we are to be missionaries of the word. When Christian preachers spread abroad the good news about Jesus, they do it with a more profound understanding of it than the shepherds and the friends of Elizabeth had. Their deeper understanding has been received in no small measure from you, Mary, who kept all these word-events and pondered them in your heart.

Your absorption in Jesus and your total consecration to him is implied in those Greek words used by Luke which are translated as "kept." "His mother kept all these words in her heart" (Luke 2:51). "Mary kept all these things, pondering them in her heart" (Luke 2:19).

"Kept" in these two sentences translates two different Greek words which are compounded from the same root word, using different intensifying prepositions. In the first case (2:51), "kept" is a translation of *diatero,* "to watch thoroughly, to observe strictly." Mary, you were no mere passive bystander at the word-events of your Son's life. You watched with all your heart, and your heart involved you in all that was taking place.

In the second case (2:19), "kept" translates *syntero,* "to keep closely together, conserve, remember, obey." The root in both of these words is *tero,* "to guard by keeping the eye upon, to fulfill a command, to hold fast, to keep."

When Luke says in a later chapter, "Blessed are they that hear the word of God and keep it" (11:28), he has in mind the picture he has already drawn of you, Mary, as the perfect hearer and keeper of the word. In this case, "keep" translates *phulasso,* "to watch, preserve, obey."

Considering all these meanings of the word kept, we may conclude that when Luke says that you kept all these word-events in your heart, he means that you watched them closely, noted them carefully, remembered them lovingly, preserved them faithfully, pondered them deeply, came to understand them thoroughly, responded to them

obediently, became completely involved in them, lived
them fully. All this is part of the continuing process of believing. Believing is lovingly receiving God's revelation
and responding to it by living according to it in love.

Mary, you were not only completely absorbed in loving contemplation of Jesus, but you responded perfectly
to him and became completely involved with him, who is
himself the word-event. He is the Word, who is both the
person revealing and the truth revealed. "He is both the
mediator of revelation and the fullness of revelation"
(Vatican II, DV 2).

You were lovingly and totally involved with the Word
himself not just in his childhood days when he still needed
you as a mother, but throughout his career, even to his
death on the cross. You are inseparably associated with
him in the fullness of faith and love.

Jesus invites us to follow you in this involvement
when he responds to the woman who cried out to him
from the crowd, "Blessed is the womb that bore you, and
the breasts that nursed you!" (Luke 11:27). He says in
reply, "Rather, blessed are they who hear the word of
God and keep it" (Luke 11:28).

Mary, you had kept his word in every sense of the
word "kept." You were able to obey the word in the fullest possible way because you had come to fullest possible
understanding of it in your loving pondering. Thus you
became totally absorbed in Jesus in love, and completly
consecrated to him and to his work. Jesus invites all of us
to this same absorption and consecration. This is expressed in St. Bede's commentary on the words of the
woman from the crowd and the response of Jesus:

>"How beautifully our Savior replies to this wom-
>an's word of witness! He points out that Mary, who
>had the merit of being bodily the mother of the Word

of God, is not the only one who is blessed. Rather, all who have striven to conceive the same word spiritually by faith, who have striven by good works to bring it to birth in their heart and in the hearts of their neighbors, and as it were to give it nourishment —all these too he proclaims blessed. For assuredly though the mother of God is blessed because she was the temporal minister of the Word's incarnation, she is far more blessed because, by ever loving him, she never ceased to be his eternal keeper" (ML 92:480).

9

THE TIMELESS VISITATION: COMMUNION
WITH MARY IN THE HOLY SPIRIT

When I watch you visiting your cousin Elizabeth, Mary, I become aware that you are visiting me as well. You become present with me in the same way that you are present with Elizabeth—in the Holy Spirit!

Your presence with Elizabeth is no mere human presence of two people in ordinary communion with each other. You are in communion with each other in the Holy Spirit.

You yourself had been filled with the Holy Spirit at the Annunciation. Impelled by him, you hasten over the hills to Elizabeth's home. Inspired by the Spirit, you greet Elizabeth. Immediately the child in Elizabeth's womb leaps for joy, and Elizabeth too is filled with the Holy Spirit. In his light, she recognizes that you are Mother of the Lord. She cries out to you in a loud voice, "Blessed are you among women, and blessed is the fruit of your womb! Why is this granted to me that the mother of my Lord should come to me?" (Luke 1:43). Only when Elizabeth has been filled with the Holy Spirit does she have the light to know that the Child in your womb is the Lord: the One who gives the Holy Spirit.

Spirit responds to Spirit. The Spirit in Elizabeth responds to the Spirit in you, the one same Holy Spirit who fills both of you. You are in communion with each other in the Holy Spirit.

Mary, the story of the Visitation is the story of your God-given power in the Spirit to visit all of us and be in communion with us.

I can understand how you can be present to me in the Holy Spirit only when I realize that all true Christians can be present to one another in the Holy Spirit. In the Holy Spirit, the Church is present to those whom she saves. But the Church is the people who are the Church. Mary, the whole Church is prefigured in your person, and thus from this mystery of your presence with Elizabeth in the Holy Spirit, we learn how the Church is present to mankind. St. Peter says of those who proclaim the word of God, "They preach the gospel to you in the power of the Holy Spirit sent from heaven" (1 Peter 1:12). Only in the power of the Holy Spirit is the Church able to speak to the hearts of men and effectively bring them to salvation.

I too, as a member of the Church and preacher of the gospel in this twentieth century, am present in the power of the Holy Spirit to the hearers of the word. My physical presence to those who listen to me, and the sound of my natural voice in their ears, would be completely worthless to them as far as salvation effects are concerned, if I were not at the same time present to them in the Holy Spirit, who speaks from my heart and speaks in their hearts. My words are ineffective for the salvation of others unless I am vivified by the Holy Spirit as I speak, and the same Holy Spirit vivifies those who hear me. I and my listeners have to be present to one another in the Holy Spirit.

And through me and the Holy Spirit, the Lord Jesus himself is present and active, touching the hearts of those who hear me.

The One Who Gives the Spirit

Mary, it is not without reason that Luke refers to the infant in your womb as the Lord (Luke 1:43), even though this is a title which was bestowed upon him only in his resurrection. His title "Lord" signifies that he is the one who gives the Holy Spirit. The Visitation story shows him already pouring out the Holy Spirit while he is still in your womb. Therefore Elizabeth calls you "Mother of my Lord."

The Lord Jesus, risen from the dead, is present everywhere in the power of his Holy Spirit. St. Paul says that the Church is "the body of Christ, the fullness of him who fills all in all" (Ephesians 1:23). He means that the Lord, as "life-giving Spirit" (1 Corinthians 15:45), fills the Church with his Holy Spirit, and through the Church fills the universe. "He who descended is he who also ascended above all the heavens that he might fill all things" (Ephesians 4:10).

Filled with his Spirit, the Church is the Body of the Lord, the extension of his incarnation, through which he carries on his own sanctifying work in the Spirit. But the Church is his people. It is the communion of saints, including those of heaven as well as those on earth. The Lord Jesus works through his whole Body and all its members. He works personally, in the power of his Spirit, through those whom he sends. Thus he exercises his lordship, his power to fill the human race with the Holy Spirit. The Church's presence would be worthless if it were not a presence to men in the power of the Holy Spirit.

As the living image of the Church, Mary, you have this power to be present to us in the Holy Spirit in a unique way. For in your person, the paschal mystery of Jesus has been brought to fulfillment in an eminent manner.

The Paschal Mystery in Us

To the extent that a person enters into our Lord's paschal mystery, he is empowered by the Holy Spirit with a share in the power of the risen Lord, Son of God in power. The paschal mystery is the mystery of our Lord's death and resurrection and sending of the Holy Spirit. As Paschal Lamb, giving his life on the cross, Jesus goes to his Father and receives the Holy Spirit from him, and pours him out into the hearts of men. When the Holy Spirit comes into our hearts, he perfects the paschal mystery in each of us, so that with Jesus we die to sin, and with Jesus we live his resurrected life in the Spirit. To the extent that we die with Jesus to sinful selfishness and enter into his loving obedience to the Father, to that extent the power of the Holy Spirit is released in our hearts, and we share in the Lord's power to be present to others in the Holy Spirit.

In your person, Mary, the paschal mystery of Jesus has been accomplished in a unique way, in the most perfect fullness possible. In a very real way you died with Jesus on Calvary. One with your Son in a perfect union of love, you suffered his agony and death with him. Because you were obedient with him even unto death, God exalted you in the grace of the Assumption, transforming you in the glory of the Lord's own resurrection. Because you were one with him in dying, and are now transformed in his glory, you are one with him in his life-giving power.

The Assumption and the Visitation

Mary, because through the grace of the Assumption you are now in the full glory of the risen Lord in heaven, you can be present with me here and now in the Holy Spirit, just as you were present with Elizabeth and Zechariah and John in that same Holy Spirit.

That is why the story of the Visitation is read in the liturgy of the feast of the Assumption. The mystery of the Visitation is the timeless mystery of your power in the Holy Spirit to be present with all of God's people as their spiritual mother, sharing in your Son's power as Lord because you shared in his obedience unto death. At your Visitation to Elizabeth, you were able to bring Jesus only to a handful of people, because, like Jesus himself, you were still subject to the human condition, and your presence was limited by place and time.

Jesus himself, before his death and resurrection, was limited by place and time, and he exercised his power only here or there as he walked from place to place in the Holy Land. But once he was transformed in the glory of his resurrection and constituted Son of God in power, he was able to fill the whole universe with his presence and power in the Holy Spirit.

You too, Mary, sharing in the fullness of his glory through the grace of the Assumption, are no longer subject to the time and place limitations of your visit to the home of Zechariah and Elizabeth, but are able to visit all mankind, your spiritual children, in the power of the Holy Spirit. You are able to visit wherever the Lord himself exercises his power in the Spirit.

As a type of the Church, in a full and exemplary way you exercise the Church's power to be present with mankind in the power of the Spirit. You share in the Lord's power in a fullness possessed by no other member of the Church, for no other member has lived the paschal mystery of Jesus with him in the uniquely perfect way in which you lived it.

Thus the mystery of the Visitation, seen in relationship with the mystery of the Assumption, shows forth the mystery of the Church's power to be present to mankind in the power of the Holy Spirit. To the extent that God's people enter into the paschal mystery of Jesus and die with him to sin and selfishness, to that extent they share in his glory and in his power to be present to their fellowmen in the Holy Spirit, and thus continue the Lord's own saving work. Mary, to deny that you can be present with us in the Holy Spirit is to deny that God's people, the Church, can be present with one another in the power of the Holy Spirit, and this is to deny the Church's power to save.

The Timeless Visitation

Thus the mystery of the Visitation, manifesting your power in the Spirit to visit each one of us, is a timeless mystery, one mystery with the mystery of the Lord's resurrection and your own assumption into his glory and power. There is special significance in Luke presenting you in the Visitation as "Mother of THE LORD." "Lord" is the title of Jesus exalted in the glory of his resurrection. The mystery of the Lord's resurrection is superimposed, as it were, on the mystery of his presence as an infant in your womb at the Visitation. Already in the womb he is called by the title of his resurrection: "Why is this granted to me that the mother of my Lord should come to me?" (Luke 1:42). In the same way, the mystery of your Assumption is superimposed on the mystery of the Visitation. The Lady visiting Elizabeth is presented in mystery as already the Lady of the Assumption into the Lord's glory, empowered to visit all of us in the Spirit.

Just as the title "Lord" is most fully verified of your Son only when he is exalted in the glory of his resurrection as Son of God with power to give the Holy Spirit, so too your title "Mother of the Lord," already true in the Visitation, is most fully verified in the Assumption, for then you are the Mother of the Lord exalted in glory.

Each one of us can now say what Elizabeth said, "Why is this granted to me, that the mother of my Lord should come to me?" For in your Assumption, you have been empowered in the Spirit to visit every one of us, and in that Holy Spirit we can live in communion with you.

Come, Mother of the Lord, visit me! Let your greeting sound in my ears, and I, like Elizabeth, will be filled with joy in the Holy Spirit! "Let me see your face, let me hear your voice, for your voice is sweet, and your face is comely!" (Song of Songs 2:14).

10

VISITATION IN LOVE

Mary, your presence with us in the Holy Spirit is a presence in love. For what happens when the Holy Spirit is poured out into our hearts and we die to sinful selfishness? We are filled with God's own love, and in his love we are present to one another.

God speaks to us not only in words, but even more eloquently in word-events, the things he does in the mysteries of salvation. Your presence with Elizabeth in the Holy Spirit was a word speaking of God's love, because God's love filled your heart and impelled you to make this visit. Elizabeth responded, to this word of love, and received the Lord who came in that love.

Mary, our spiritual mother, you come to us in that same love, winning the same kind of response from our hearts, drawing us to the Lord who is manifest in your visitation to us.

It is the very nature of love to want to be present with those we love. Your fullness of love for us as our spiritual mother, inspired by the fullness of the Holy Spirit in your heart, impels you to visit us who are in need of your motherly attenion and care.

If we are to benefit fully from your loving presence, we must live in our own lives what we see in yours. Help us therefore to consider more deeply how you are present with us in love, so that we can be present to others in that way, in the Holy Spirit.

How shall we put it, Mary? Are you present with me in the Holy Spirit, or is the Holy Spirit present to me in you? That is, does your visit to me begin in your own initiative, or does it begin in the Spirit's initiative?

It begins in the Spirit's initiative, but it also begins in yours, for you and the Holy Spirit have become one spirit. "He who is united to the Lord becomes one Spirit with him" (1 Corinthians (6:17). No one is more closely united to the Lord than you, his mother. If it can be said of anyone, it can be said of you, that you are one body, one Spirit with the Lord (Ephesians 4:4-5).

The Holy Spirit loves me so much that he wishes to manifest his presence with me, and so he comes to me in your love for me. For he is the unseen One, and becomes visibly present in the love of Christians for one another. And so your love for me and presence with me reveals his presence with me. When you come to me in the Spirit's power, the Holy Spirit comes in you. And where the Spirit is, Father and Son are there, too, for he is their love, given to me.

God himself is really present to those whom I love with the love which he pours out into my heart in giving me the Holy Spirit (Romans 5:5). For Jesus said to me, "As the Father has loved me, so have I loved you... As I have loved you, love one another" (John 15:9, 12). One same love is given by the Father to the Son, and communicated to us by the Son in the Holy Spirit.

When Jesus tells us to love "as" the Father loves, and as he himself loves, the word "as" means more than "like." It means that we are to love with his very own love, just as he loves with the Father's love. Our love for one another has its source in the Lord's love for us, just as his love for us has its source in the Father's love for him. It is one same love in the Holy Spirit in which the

Father and Son love each other and us, and in which we love them, and one another.

I myself still fall short in obeying this command to love with God's own love, for the Lord's work of transforming me into himself is not yet finished. I am not yet perfectly one Spirit with him, for I am still a sinner. But you, Mary, cannot fall short in keeping this command, now that the paschal mystery is completed in you. For you are transformed into the Lord's glory, and in the fullest possible meaning of the words, are "one Spirit with the Lord."

Therefore God is really present with me in your presence to me. For in the love for me which he has inspired in your heart, his own love is actively present with me.

That is why I can say it either way, Mary. You are present with me in the Holy Spirit, and the Holy Spirit is present with me in you. Your visit to me begins in the Holy Spirit's initiative, and begins in your initiative, for you and he love me as one Spirit, with one love. You are present to me in the Holy Spirit, and your presence with me in his power springs from your love for me. And the Holy Spirit is present to me in you, for your presence with me springs from his love for me. You and the Lord love me as one. The Lord Jesus is present with me in his Spirit through your presence with me.

In you, Mother, the Lord manifests what he wants to accomplish in all of us. He wants all of us to be vessels of his own love and presence to all our fellowmen. To deny these things of you is to deny their possibility in our own lives. You are ever a presence and manifestation of the Holy Spirit, who reveals in you what he wills to do in me.

When I look at you in the Annunciation scene, or watch you in your visit with Elizabeth, your presence with me draws forth from my heart a flash of faith and love reaching out to you and to the infant Lord in your womb. For his presence through you in these timeless mysteries is a perpetual revelation of his closeness to me. In you, Mary, God has become visibly present on earth!

PART II

the mother of jesus:

at cana and calvary

11

THE MOTHER OF JESUS

O Mary, our Mother, the disciple whom Jesus loved knew that your name was Mary, and he knew that his own name was John. Yet throughout his gospel he never calls you Mary, and he never calls himself John. Instead, he uses symbolic names which indicate special vocations within the Lord's own work. He refers to himself only as "the disciple whom Jesus loved" (John 13:23; 19:26; 21:7). And he calls you only "the Mother of Jesus" (John 2:1; 19:25-26).

John uses these two titles almost as if they were proper names. In calling himself simply "the disciple whom Jesus loved," he is presenting himself as the symbol of every faithful disciple of the Lord. Therefore he wants me to see myself in this symbol. And in calling you "the Mother of Jesus," he means far more than the immediately evident sense of the words. You are not merely the one who formed Jesus in your womb. You are mother also of all those in whom Jesus lives. You form Jesus in the hearts of the disciples. Thus, "Mother of Jesus" indicates not only your relationship with Jesus, but also your maternal relationship with all of us, who are symbolized in "the disciple whom Jesus loved."

Jesus indicates this extended relationship when he speaks to you and to John from the cross. "When Jesus saw his mother and the disciple whom he loved standing near, he said to his mother, 'Woman, behold your son!' Then he said to the disciple, 'Behold your mother!' " (John 19:26).

Mother, in pondering these words to fathom their depths, I have to be aware of John's ways of speaking. I notice how more than once in his gospel, he presents scenes like this in which a messenger of God sees a person and says, "Behold!" In each case the messenger goes on to give a description revealing the mission of the person indicated. John the Baptist, for example, sees Jesus and says, "Behold the Lamb of God, who takes away the sin of the world" (John 1:29). Likewise Pilate, not knowing the profound meaning of what he is saying, presents Jesus crowned with thorns and says, "Behold your king!" (John 19:14). Thus, in John's gospel, "Behold" introduces a formula of revelation.[1]

Using this formula as he hangs on the cross, Jesus is revealing something concerning you, Mother. He sees you standing with the disciple whom he loves, and says, "Woman, behold your son." And to the disciple he says, "Behold your mother." Thus he reveals you as mother of all the faithful, and he reveals our relationship to you as your spiritual children.

To grasp fully the significance of this scene for me personally, I have to be deeply conscious of what John means throughout his gospel in calling himself "the disciple whom Jesus loved." John has experienced the truth of what Jesus said to all his disciples: "As the father has loved me, so have I loved you; abide in my love" (John 15:9). He has experienced the Lord's intimate personal love for him, and he responds to that love and remains in it. The Lord's love is pure gift: "You did not choose me, but I chose you" (John 15:16). Thus, a true disciple, a faithful believer, is one who receives and accepts the gift of love and abides in it.

---

[1]Raymond E. Brown, The Gospel According to John (New York: Doubleday, 1966, 1970), p. 58, 923.

Receiving God's Love

Believing is receiving. It is receiving God's love and his life, given to us in the Son: "God so loved the world that he gave his only Son, that whoever believes in him should not perish, but have eternal life" (John 3:16). Believing is receiving the only Son, and it is receiving divine sonship in him: "To all who received him by believing in his name, he gave power to become sons of God" (John 1:12). Believing is receiving God's gift of living waters, the life in the Spirit given by Jesus: "If you knew the gift of God, and who it is that is saying to you, 'Give me a drink,' you would have asked him, and he would have given you living water" (John 4:10).

Mary, this gift of God's love, this gift of divine sonship, this life in the Spirit, is the life given to every true disciple. This life in us is entrusted by Jesus to you as our spiritual mother. Receiving you as my mother is part of the process of receiving the fullness of love and life which God gives me in Jesus his Son.

I receive you as my mother with the same divine faith and love in which I receive Jesus as Son of God, and become son or daughter of God in him. I accept you as my mother just as the disciple did. "From that hour," the hour of the paschal sacrifice of Jesus the Lamb, "the disciple *received* her into his own" (John 19:27). John means that he opened his heart to you as his mother.

I know that this is what John meant, for the word "received" which he uses is the same word he used in writing, "To all who received him by believing in his name, he gave power to become children of God" (John 1:12). Again and again in his gospel John uses this word in speaking of the gifts of God which we receive in faith and love. Believing, we receive God's testimony (3:11), his word (17:8), his Spirit (14:17), and especially the Word, his Son (1:12), and all that flows from the Son's fullness (1:16).

O Mother of Jesus, you too are to be received as God's gift of love to us. Like the disciple who received you into his own, accepting you into his heart in faith and love, Jesus would have all of us receive you as our own mother, in the same faith and love in which we receive him personally.

Mother of the Life in Jesus

In calling you "the Mother of Jesus," John means far more than that you are the one who gave Jesus his human life. In John's thinking, Jesus is more than the man and God whom you formed in your womb and brought into the world. Throughout his gospel, John is telling us that your Son Jesus is complete and total only when he lives in his disciples and they live in him, in such a way that they are all one in him. "I am the vine, you are the branches; abide in me and I in you" (John 15:4-5).

A vine and its branches is one living thing. Jesus and his disciples are like one living person. This is a persistent theme in John gospel. Jesus is "the *only* Son" (John 1:14), and others can be children of God only in him, sharing in his life (John 1:12). Apart from him or outside of him we are not children of God. "Apart from me you can do nothing" (John 15:5). "No one comes to the Father but by me" (John 14:6).

All to whom he gives divine life are one with him in his own life with the Father: "Father, I have given them the glory you gave me, that they may be one as we are one" (John 17:22). The Father loves the disciples with the same love with which he loves Jesus: "Father, that the love with which you love me may be in them, and I in them" (John 17:26).

God has only one Son, Jesus. And only in him, as one with him, are we God's sons and daughters. Mary, Mother of Jesus, you too have only one Son, Jesus. And we are your sons and daughters in him, and in no other way.

Only in the context of John's whole gospel, then, do we know what Jesus meant when he said to you, "Woman, behold your Son." We understand in what sense you are mother of "the disciple whom Jesus loved." You are mother of Jesus living in each of his disciples. You are mother of all those whom he takes into his own divine sonship. Jesus himself is completed only in those in whom he lives. You are mother of all those to whom Jesus gives his life in the Holy Spirit. Living in the Spirit, they are God's sons and daughters, and have one Father with Jesus: "I am ascending to my Father and your Father, to my God and your God" (John 20:17). You are mother of all who call God "Father."

You are spiritual mother of the whole Christ, head and members, vine and branches. You are the mother of Jesus living in all who are one with him, going to the Father in him, sharing in the one life of the only Son of God.

Thus, the proper name which John gives you— "Mother of Jesus"—signifies your vocation as mother of the whole Christ. It is your vocation in the Church, and with the Church, to form the life of Jesus in each of his members, so that all may be one in him. You are the mother who forms the Mystical Body of Jesus, the Church.

In the womb of your love, Mother, form Christ in us! All the family of God's children live together in Jesus, and you are his mother, and mother of all who are in him. Form all of us in Christian unity!

"Woman," Mother of the Disciple

Therefore, Mother, when Jesus sees John standing with you at the cross and says to him, "Behold your mother," he is not simply performing a son's act of reverence towards his mother. A few minutes later you will be childless as well as widowed. But Jesus is not merely giving you into the care of someone who will be a son to you, filling the void left in you by his own death. No, the whole literary structure of John's crucifixion scene is so pregnant with rich theological meaning that we are forced to see something far more profound than this in your Son's words to you and to John. The title "Woman" is an integral part of the revelation formula used by Jesus in saying, "Woman, behold your Son."

In calling you "Woman," Jesus shows that in "the hour" of his paschal sacrifice, he wishes to reveal you as the woman you are in God's plan, he wants to show your vocation within his own redeeming work. He calls you "Woman" each time he speaks to you in John's gospel (John 2:4; 19:26). Thus he indicates that the woman theme running throughout the Scriptures is fulfilled in you. According to the mysterious design of God, you are intimately connected with the death and glorification of your Son. As "the Woman," you are established in the function of Mother of "the disciple." It is striking and significant that Jesus refers to you as "mother" only in relationship to the disciple whom he loves, the symbol of all believers: "Behold your mother!" (John 19:27).

In never saying "Mother" to you, but addressing you only as "Woman," Jesus seems to be indicating his inevitable separation from you, and the necessity that you die to what is most truly yourself, your motherhood of Jesus. The sword of sorrow pierces you in what is most dear to you. Along with your Son on the cross, you must die, as mother. He must part from you in death.

This dying of your motherhood begins long before Calvary. Each time Jesus speaks to you throughout the gospels, he seems to be putting you aside, indicating the inevitable separation which will take place at the cross. The sword of sorrow announced to you by Simeon is always at work. Already after his first separation from you when he is twelve years old, Jesus foreshadows the separation to be accomplished on Calvary, saying, "Did you not know that I must be in my Father's house?" (Luke 2:49). He goes to the Father's house only by way of the cross. And at Cana he says to you, seemingly rejecting you from his mission, "Woman, what is that to me and to you?" (John 2:4).

But in this separation accomplished in his death, this dying to your maternity, you become Mother in a marvelous new way. In the person of the disciple whom he loves, Jesus entrusts every true believer to you, and you become mother to all believers.

Thus your Son consecrates you in his own death, as "mother of all the living" (Genesis 3:20), and therefore as "the Woman," the New Eve, the true Daughter of Zion whose mystery was gradually unfolded in the Old Testament.

Behold Your Mother!

Lord Jesus, your words are spirit and life! (John 6:63). They are like a two-edged sword piercing our hearts (Hebrews 4:12).

If this is true of all your words, is it any less true of the words you spoke from the cross? Would not your last words somehow be even more piercing, more life-giving than any of the others? Is there not somehow a special power in those words you spoke when you said to me from the cross, "Behold your mother" (John 19:27)?

You meant these words for me personally, for I am the disciple whom you loved (John 19:29). For "the disciple whom Jesus loved" is the symbol of every true believer, everyone who has been pierced to the heart by your words.

Lord, your words are always creative. They call into being what did not exist before. "By the word of the Lord the heavens were made. . . He spoke and the earth came to be" (Psalm 33:6, 9). You said, "Let there be light," and there was light! (Gen. 1:3). You said to the leper, "Be clean! and immediately the leprosy left him (Mark 1:41). You said to the dead daughter of Jairus, "Little girl, I say to you, arise!" and the little girl stood up, alive and hungry (Mark 5:41-43).

Your word is ever true. It not only expresses truth, but makes things to be true. You said, "This is my body," and therefore it *is* your body (Mark 14:22). You said, "This is my blood of the covenant," and therefore it *is* your blood (Mark 14:24).

You said to me, "This is your mother" (John 19:27), and therefore your mother *is* my mother. You said to her indicating me, "This is your son" (John 19:26), and so I *am* her son.

Your power-filled word is never spoken in vain. You said, "My word that goes forth from my mouth shall not return to me void, but shall do my will, achieving the end for which I sent it" (Isa. 55:11). Your word is in vain unless you speak it personally in the heart of each one of us. You must speak it to me personally if it is to create life in me. You have spoken in my heart, "Behold your mother," and that is why I have come to Mary my Mother in love.

No one can come to her in the way you would have us come to her, unless the Father draws him to her through your life-giving word (Cf. John 6:44). Your word to Mary concerning me, "Behold your son" (John 19:26), can take full effect only when you say to me personally, "Behold your mother" (John 19:27), drawing me to her by the power of your word and Spirit.

Speak that word daily anew in my heart! Draw me infallibly to your mother in filial love! To be fully her child is to be fully responsive to your mother. Only when I am responsive to your mother in reverential love can she be fully my mother, for only then am I fully open to her life-giving maternal influence.

Lord Jesus, may the words of this book be your own life-giving word! Give Spirit and life to every word I write. Through my words, pierce the hearts of my readers, saying to them, "Behold your mother!" May these pages be an experience of you personally introducing the readers to your mother. Lord, through my words, say to them of her, "This is my mother. Love her as your own mother, so that you and I may be brothers and sisters born of the same mother, just as we have the same Father in heaven."

12

MARY, TYPE OF THE CHURCH

A Sword Shall Pierce

How fascinating it must have been for you, Mary, to watch your Son Jesus grow, and to look for the clues which hinted to you who he really was, and what was the mission entrusted to him. You treasured all the words spoken about him, "pondering them in your heart" (Luke 2:19).

At the Presentation. the prophet Simeon told you that Jesus was "a light for revelation to the Gentiles" (Luke 2:32). In saying this, Simeon was quoting from the Servant Poems of Isaiah (Isaiah 42:6; 49:6). Thus he informed you that Jesus is the Servant of Yahweh: "Behold my servant . . . in whom my soul delights . . . a light to the nations" (Isaiah 42:1-6). God delights in the Servant because he will accomplish God's will to save all the nations.

Surely, Mary, you must have followed this clue given by Simeon all the way through. Did you discover the rest that Isaiah says about the Servant: that he will be "a man of sorrows, and acquainted with grief? (Isaiah 53:3)? Simeon had told you, "A sword will pierce through your own soul also" (Luke 2:35). You must have realized that this prediction would be fulfilled in your close association with your Son, the Man of Sorrows: "He was pierced for our offenses, crushed for our sins" (Isaiah 53:5).

Mary, you loved to ponder God's word. You and Jesus must have reflected together on the Scriptures in your home at Nazareth. As you pondered with him what you heard in the synagogue, did not the Holy Spirit enlighten you as well as Jesus? The human mind of Jesus was coming to a fuller understanding of himself in the light of these Scriptures. With Jesus, did you not notice and understand Isaiah's words about the Servant, that "if he gives his life as an offering for sin . . . the will of the Lord shall be accomplished through him" (Isaiah 53:10)?

How many people today receive direct personal enlightenment from the Holy Spirit when they read the Scriptures! Did the Spirit speak any less to you when you pondered the Scriptures than he does to us? He must have given you many profound insights into the passion of Jesus even before he suffered.

Jesus came to this understanding, and was able to explain in advance why he would die. Isaiah had said of him, "If he *gives his life* as an offering for sin . . . through his suffering my servant will justify many" (Isaiah 53:10-11). Jesus was clearly referring to these words of the prophet when he said of himself, "The Son of Man came not to be served, but to serve, and to *give his life* as a ransom for many" (Mark 10:45).

Surely, Mary, insights like this must have sustained your courage as you stood at the cross of Jesus. Because you knew, along with Jesus, that the Servant Poems described the mission of Jesus, you could generously endure the sword of sorrow which Simeon had predicted for you. You endured it for love of us, "for he was pierced for our offenses, crushed for our sins, upon him was the chastisement that makes us whole, by his stripes we were healed" (Isaiah 53:5).

Since you knew at the cross, Mary, that Jesus was suffering for us and that you were suffering with him for us, we can understand why Jesus would say to you, indicating us, "Woman, behold your son" (John 19:26). It was as if he said to you, "Your suffering for them with me is not in vain. In these sufferings they are born to new life!"

Your love which suffered so for us will never abandon us! When we in turn will have to suffer in the likeness of your Son (Romans 8:17), you will support us as you supported him. O Mother, stand with us when we are nailed to the cross with Jesus!

Type of the Church

Mother, just as you followed up the clues which God's word gave you concerning your Son, so the Fathers of the Church followed up the scriptural clues about you. Pondering these in the light of the Holy Spirit, they came to an ever deeper understanding of you as type and symbol of God's people, the Church. Their reflection must have run something like this:

Why did Jesus, at Cana and at Calvary, address you as "Woman"? Why did he not affectionately call you "Mother"?

He called you "Woman" to indicate that the biblical theme of the Woman finds its fulfillment in you as type of the Church.

The theme of the Woman begins in Genesis and runs through the Scriptures all the way to the Book of Revelation. The Lord God said to the serpent, "I will make you enemies of each other: you and the woman, your offspring and her offspring. It will crush your head, and you will strike its heel" (Genesis 3:15). Who is this woman whose offspring will crush Satan?

Again and again in the Old Testament, God's people were personified as a woman. Thus Zephaniah addresses Israel, "Rejoice . . . O daughter of Jerusalem! . . . Do not fear, O Zion . . . the Lord, your God is in your midst" (Zephaniah 3:14-17). Mary, did you realize at the Annunciation that Zephaniah's words to Daughter Jerusalem are deliberately echoed by Gabriel's words to you: "Rejoice, O favored one, the Lord is with you. . . . Do not be afraid, Mary, for you have found favor with God" (Luke 1:28,30)?

Luke thus describes you, Mary, in the same words in which the Scriptures describe Daughter Jerusalem, the personification of God's people. In this way he indicates that you are the Woman in whom all the promises of God to his people are fulfilled. You are the type and representative of the whole people of God.

In the story of the Visitation, Luke continues to present you as the personification of God's people. Elizabeth's words to you, *"Blessed are you among women, and blessed is the fruit of your womb"* (Luke 1:42), are a clear echo of the blessing addressed to Judith, who is a personification of the Jewish people:

> *Blessed are you, daughter, by the Most High God above all the women on earth, and blessed be the Lord God, the creator of heaven and earth, who guided your blow at the head of the chief of our enemies* (Judith 13:18).

These words about Judith's blow at the enemy's head bring to mind at once the woman in Genesis whose offspring will crush the head of the serpent (Genesis 3:15). Holofernes, whose head is cut off by Judith, symbolizes all the powers of evil crushed by God's people. Judith, whose name means "Jewess," symbolizes God's people receiving the blessings promised to Abraham, their father. The crushing of the forces of evil is in fulfillment of these blessings.

Therefore the blessing addressed to Judith is deliberately patterned upon the blessing pronounced by Melchizedek over Abraham after his defeat of the four kings:

> *Blessed be Abram by God Most High, the creator of heaven and earth, and blessed be God Most High, who has delivered your enemies into your hand!* (Genesis 14:19).

By letting the blessings of Abraham and of Judith echo in Elizabeth's words of blessing addressed to you, Mary, the Holy Spirit is telling us that all the blessings promised to Abraham and his people are granted to us in Jesus, the blessed fruit of your womb. Blessed among women, you are the Woman in whose person God's people crush the enemy, as Holofernes was crushed through Judith.

In turn, Mary, you are a prefiguring of God's people, the Church, who are empowered by Jesus to crush all the powers of evil: "The God of peace will soon crush Satan under your feet!" (Romans 16:20).

The Woman in Labor

Again, in the prophet Micah, God's people in their sufferings are personified as a woman in the pains of childbirth, bringing forth a redeemed people. "Writhe in pain, grow faint, O daughter Zion, like a woman in travail" (Micah 4:10). The prophet continues, showing how the sufferings of God's people will be turned into blessing when the mother of the Messiah brings forth her Son:

"The Lord will give them up until the time when she who is to give birth has borne" (Micah 5:2).

Luke is referring to these words of Micah when he says of you, Mary, "The time came for her to be delivered, and she gave birth to her firstborn son" (Luke 2:6). In your person, Mary, God's suffering people brings forth a Savior (Cf. Revelation 12:5).

Isaiah, a contemporary of Micah, also speaks of a mysterious Woman: "The virgin shall be with child, and bear a son, and shall name him Emmanuel" (Isaiah 7:14). Along with St. Matthew, the Church has always seen these words of Isaiah fulfilled in your virginal conception of Jesus, by the overshadowing of the Holy Spirit (Matthew 1:18-24). Just as the Spirit of the Lord moved over the abyss at the first creation (Genesis 1:2), so his overshadowing of you with the power of God is the beginning of the new creation in Christ, conceived in your womb. Creation, tainted by sin, had to have a new beginning, spotless and virginal, and God brings this about in you, O blessed virgin Mary, who conceive your child by the power of the Holy Spirit.

Mary: Corporate Personality

Mother, in presenting you as a personification of God's people, Luke gave the Church a valuable clue for coming to an understanding of herself. The Fathers of the Church quickly took up the clue, and called you "type of the Church." By coming to an understanding of you, God's people would come to a deeper understanding of themselves.

As type of the Church, Mary, you are a corporate personality.[1] The word 'corporate" is derived from the Latin for body. A corporate personality is a leader who acts as head of a body of people. Because the leader acts for the people as their representative, the whole people acts in his person. But what the leader has first accomplished in his own person on behalf of all, each of his people must in turn ratify and carry out in their own person.

Jesus is a corporate personality. What he did for us in his life on earth and on the cross, each of us must now do in our own person by the power of his grace and headship.

You, too, Mary, are a corporate personality. You do not stand apart from the Church, but are one body with it. In your response to the Lord, you do not act simply as a private individual, but as a person representing the whole body. At the Annunciation, the whole people of God is present in your person as their representative, and you act in their behalf in listening to God's word and giving your response. The Church first comes to its perfection in your person through your perfect response at the Annunciation and through your continuing response to the Lord Jesus throughout your life with him, all the way to the cross.

What you did in your relationship with the Lord as representative of God's whole people, each of these people must now do in their own person, in your likeness. Thus, under your real maternal influence, the rest of the Church comes to the perfection which is already accomplished in you.

As type of the Church, you are not simply an image or likeness of the Church, but you are also the very beginning of the Church: the Church already exists and is perfect in your person. You are a symbol because the reality symbolized has already been completed in you. In your person, God has first accomplished all that he intends to accomplish in turn in the rest of his people. Thus you are the living image of our hope. You are the pledge and promise of all that God intends for all of us. You are the revelation of what God will do for all of us, if, in our own person, we respond to him in the way that you responded to him on our behalf.

"The Woman" at the Cross

The title "Woman" belongs to you most fully, Mary, as you stand at the cross of Jesus when his "hour" has come. Jesus compares his own sufferings on the cross, and the sufferings of his followers, to the sufferings of a woman in childbirth when her "hour" has come. "When a woman is in travail, she has sorrow, because her hour has come, but when she is delivered of her child, she no longer remembers the anguish, for joy that a man is born into the world" (John 16:21). Jesus says that a man, not a child, is born, because Jesus and his Church in their sufferings bring forth the new mankind restored to the image of its Creator (Colossians 3:10).

Mary, when Jesus addresses you at Cana as "Woman," and directs your attention to his "hour" of sufferings on the cross (John 2:4), he is telling you that you will be involved in his hour. His hour is also your hour: "her hour has come" (John 16:21). It is the hour in which the Woman, God's people, represented by you, brings forth salvation, because the Messiah suffers as one with them and makes their sufferings fruitful. Suffering with Jesus at the cross, Mary, you are the representative of all God's people, and in your person, we are all there at the cross, suffering as one with Jesus.

If your Son had not come to suffer with us, all our sufferings would have been completely in vain. The fruitlessness of human sufferings without Jesus is dramatized by the prophet Isaiah:

> As a woman about to give birth writhes and cries out in her pains, so were we in your presence, O Lord. We conceived and writhed in pain, giving birth to nothing but wind; salvation we have not achieved for the earth, the inhabitants of the world cannot bring it forth (Isaiah 26:17).

Without Christ, we give birth to nothing but wind!

But Second Isaiah dramatizes even more strikingly the fruitfulness of his people's sufferings when the Messiah suffers with them, giving birth to the new mankind:

> Before she comes to labor, she gives birth; before the pains come upon her, she safely delivers a male child. Who ever heard of such a thing, or saw the like? . . . Zion is scarcely in labor when she gives birth to her children (Isaiah 66:7-8).

This image of the marvelous, joyful fruitfulness of "the Woman" is not the denial of her messianic sufferings. The prophet is simply saying what Jesus will say later: when the woman's hour has passed, she will forget her pains as though they had never been, so marvelous is the fruit she brings forth and so great is her joy in the new mankind (John 16:20-22).

Mary, your presence at the cross as "the Woman," type of the Church, shows that God's people must all share in the Lord's sufferings. But the sorrow will quickly be forgotten when the new mankind is born into the glory of the risen Lord. This is expressed in the liturgy for the Feast of your Sorrows (September 15): "O God, with Mary, your Church shared in Christ's passion. Grant that it may be worthy to share also in his resurrection" (Opening Prayer). "As we honor Mary's love which suffered with Jesus, may we make up in our own lives whatever is lacking in the sufferings of Christ, for the good of the Church" (Colossians 1:24) (Prayer after Communion).

Because we have been baptized into Christ and become one body with him, our whole life is now his life and he lives in us (Romans 6:3-4). Therefore too our sufferings are his, and he suffers in us, making our sufferings purifying and fruitful for our salvation (Romans 8:17).

On the cross "he bore our infirmities" (Isaiah 53:4), not as a sheer substitute for us so that we would not have to suffer, but that he might suffer with us and in us, and give value to whatever we endure for him, just as he gives value and fruitfulness to our joys and to whatever good we do.

Hence the joy of the infant John leaping in Elizabeth's womb, and your joy, Mary, in bringing forth Jesus at Bethlehem. Because the Savior has suffered with us and for us, every child born of woman can be born into the joy of the risen Lord.

The Beginning of the Birthpangs

The Church suffers with her divine Bridegroom in bringing forth the new creation. These sufferings of the Church began in your person, Mary, as you suffered with Jesus on the cross. The passion and death of Jesus is referred to in the Scriptures as "birthpangs" (Acts 2:24): "God raised him up, having loosed the birthpangs of death, because it was not possible for him to be held by it" (Acts 2:24). Speaking of the sufferings of his people which they would have to endure in the early days of the Church, Jesus said, "All this is only the beginning of the birthpangs" (Matthew 24:8). The birthpangs will include all the sufferings of his people in the whole era of the Church, beginning with his own sufferings on the cross and your sufferings along with his, Mary, and extending till his coming in glory. The Church will suffer with her Lord till the end of time.

And therefore in Revelation, "the Woman" is presented in glory with the risen Lord, "clothed with the sun" (Revelation 12:1), and simultaneously in birthpangs bringing forth the Messiah and "the rest of her offspring" (Revelation 12:5, 17). Just as the Church began her sufferings with her crucified Lord in your person, Mary, as you stood at the foot of the cross, so the Church has begun her glory in your person assumed into heaven and "clothed with the sun," the glory of the risen Jesus. In your glory in the assumption, you are a pledge of glory for the whole Body of Christ, the Church.

Therefore we sing to the Father in the Preface of the Mass on the Feast of your Assumption: "Today the Virgin Mother of God was taken up into heaven, to be the beginning and the pattern of the Church in its perfection, and a sign of hope and comfort for your people on their pilgrim way." Both in your sufferings and in your glory, Mary, you are inseparable from the Church. In you the Church has its beginnings, and in you it first reaches its perfection. The woman clothed in the sun, and yet in birthpangs, is the Church, and it is you. "The Woman" is the one Body of Christ in which he continues his own life, death and resurrection. You are forever the foremost member of this Body, Mary.

13

CANA AND THE WINE OF THE SPIRIT

Mother, you say to Jesus, "They have no wine." But what is Jesus trying to tell you when he says in reply, "Woman, what is that to me and to you? My hour has not yet come" (John 2:4)?

"What is that to me and to you" is a Hebrew way of speaking in which the speaker refuses to be involved in what the other proposes. Your Son's words therefore mean, "Woman, how does this concern of yours involve me?" (John 2:24,n). He is refusing your request.

If Jesus is refusing your request, why do you take it for granted that he will change his mind and do what you have asked him? Why do you go about preparing for the miracle of the wine, saying to the servants, "Do whatever he tells you"?

Mother, the wonderful persistence of your faith, in spite of your Son's refusal of your request, is so like the persistence of the Canaanite woman (Matthew 15:22). Jesus refuses her also, at first, when she asks him to free her daughter from the demon. He says to her, "It is not fair to take the children's bread and throw it to the dogs." But the woman will not take "No" for an answer. Persisting with her request, she says, "Yes, Lord, yet even the dogs eat the crumbs that fall from their master's table."

The Canaanite woman's persevering faith wins your Son's heart and makes him change his mind. He praises her persistence and grants her request: "O woman, great is your faith! Be it done for you as you desire!"

Mary, your faith too is great! Far from giving up hope because of your Son's initial refusal, you expect him to do for you what you ask. And your faith is rewarded with a magnificent answer surpassing all your expectations. Jesus provides wine of the highest quality in an amazing quantity: at least one hundred and twenty gallons! (John 2:6). Your Son's love always gives more and better than we can dream of asking. "He is able to do far more abundantly than all we ask or think!" (Ephesians 3:20).

Obviously, Mary, the Lord's extraordinary generosity in providing this abundant excellence of wine is more than a response to the need you pointed out to him. Clearly, it is a sign of the greater things which he will give when his hour comes.

His Hour

His words to you, Mary, "What is this to me and to you," amount to saying, "We have greater things to be concerned about than this shortage of wine." In adding, "My hour has not yet come," he gives you the clue to what these greater things are. He directs your attention, and ours, to the paschal mystery, 'the hour" of his passing out of this world to the Father (John 13:1), the hour of his glorification when he is lifted up on the cross: "Father, the hour has come! Glorify your Son so that the Son may glorify you" (John 17:1).

Mother, in pointing to his hour, Jesus gives you something new to ponder. He is again calling your attention to his Father's business (Luke 2:49). His whole life is regulated by his Father's will, to which he ever conforms himself. "The Son can do nothing of his own accord, but only what he sees the Father doing" (John 5:19). He always consults the Father before he does anything. "The hour" set by his Father has not yet come.

If the hour has not yet come, does this mean that Jesus does not have to be concerned with it at this moment? Is he free to enjoy this wedding and help make it a joyous occasion? Is "the hour" irrelevant to the wedding?

The Lord's "hour" of sacrifice has relevance for every detail of human life. He came to sanctify, by his paschal sacrifice, all that is human.

As Jesus reflects upon the relevance of his hour to this wedding, Mary, he finds, besides your persistent faith, another excellent reason for granting your request. He sees, on second thought, that his Father wills that he respond to your request and give you the wine for the wedding. The wine will be a symbol of more wonderful things to come. The miracle will be a sign indicating the deeper meaning of his hour. It will be a pledge of the wonderful fruits the hour will produce.

Mother, in answer to your request, Jesus thus provides infinitely more than wine! He begins to open up to all of us the mystery of his life—who he is, and what he is for us. "This, the first of his signs, Jesus did at Cana in Galilee, and manifested his glory" (John 2:11). His glory manifest at Cana is but a sign foreshadowing the glory of his hour, his glory in being lifted up in death and resurrection and giving the Holy Spirit, the fruit of his hour (John 7:39; 8:28; 12:32-33).

Here at Cana, Mother, Jesus grants you your request, as a sign and pledge that when his hour has been accomplished, he will pour out upon all of us, again at your request, the fruit of his hour, the new wine of the Holy Spirit.

The New Eve

Mother, when the hour has come, and you stand at the foot of the cross, once again your Son calls you "Woman," just as he did at Cana. In this way he indicates to us the connection between Cana and Calvary. Cana is a parable in action, interpreting for us the events of Calvary. The Lord's granting of the miracle of Cana at your request is a sign prefiguring your own involvement in the mystery of his hour. By calling you "Woman" on both occasions, he indicates that you are the New Eve.

He himself is the Second Adam (1 Corinthians 15:45) who gives life to the world through his sufferings. Because you are involved with him in the mystery of his sufferings, you are "mother of all the living" (Genesis 3:20).

Therefore when he says to you, "Woman, behold your son," by this word he creates you as the new Eve, entrusting to your maternal care all those born of water and the Spirit. For his own work on earth is now completed. The beloved disciple tells us what Jesus said and did just after his last words to you and to the disciple. "Jesus exclaimed, 'It is finished!' And bowing his head, he handed over the spirit" (John 19:30). In surrendering his human spirit to his Father in death, he hands over to us his divine Spirit, as the fruit of that death. And you were standing there, Mary, as type and representative of all of God's people, receiving this Holy Spirit for us.

In this Holy Spirit, we are all born again to the new life, with you as our mother. Just as through your intercession Jesus gave us the symbolic wine at Cana, so now through your intercession he gives us the Holy Spirit which it symbolized. In your faith at Cana and at Calvary, the faith of the Church receiving the Holy Spirit is already operative.

For in your person as corporate personality, the Church, all of God's people, is already present at the cross. In you, and as one with you, the Church too is the New Eve, "mother of all the living." As one with you, the Church is our mother. "Through the Holy Spirit," says St. Leo the Great, "Jesus himself was born of a virgin mother, and through that same Spirit, Jesus fecundates his all-pure Church, so that through the child-bearing of baptism a countless multitude of children might be born of God" (PL 54:355).

Mary, we are all your children, for we become one body with Jesus your Son through the maternal activity of the Church in baptism. Through the work of the Church, you are completing in each one of us your own maternal work which began at the Annunciation, and which was perfected on Calvary when you brought us forth in the pains of suffering. Just as the Church as mother was present at the foot of the cross in your person, so you as mother are present and active in all that Mother Church is doing in forming Jesus your Son in us. For you, along with all the saints, are forever one with the Church. You are the first and most influential member of that Church, which always works as a whole because it is the indivisible Body of your Son, through which he brings his own work to completion.

O Mother, look upon us in our neediness! Present us to your Son and say to him as you did at Cana, "They have no wine! They need the Holy Spirit!" Just as the Holy Spirit overshadowed you at the Annunciation and formed the Son of God in your womb, so now in the womb of your love for us, the Spirit forms us as sons and daughters in your Son. Protect and nourish us in the womb of your love, until we are born into the fullness of glory!

Jesus manifested his glory in the miracle at Cana, prefiguring the glory of his resurrection. The Spirit opens to our hearts the glory of Christ Jesus. Mother, obtain for us the wine of the Spirit, that we may all see the Lord's glory! (John 2:11). Show us your Son's glory! (John 17:24).

The Wine of the Spirit

O Mother, Jesus does not grant your request at Cana until he has directed your attention to the hour of his paschal mystery, the hour of his giving of the Holy Spirit. Thus he indicates to us that he answers prayer only in the context of "the hour." The hour means his paschal mystery, his going to the Father by way of the cross, to obtain for us the Holy Spirit. He grants our requests only if we present them to him within his paschal sacrifice, offering them in his Name.

His Name signifies not only who he is, but also what he has done for us in his paschal mystery. To ask in his Name is to ask in his paschal sacrifice. "If you ask anything in my Name, I will do it" (John 14:14).

And by answering your request at Cana in a way surpassing all your expectations, Mary, Jesus indicates that every request offered within his paschal sacrifice is likewise granted in a way exceeding all our desires and hopes. As the fruit of his hour he gives greater things than we would ever have dreamed of asking. The most excellent fruit of that hour is the Holy Spirit, whom he pours out to us in the blood and water from his side, and in the wine of the Holy Eucharist.

Therefore, before granting your request at Cana, Mary, Jesus directs your attention to the hour of his sacrifice, to indicate to all of us that the gift he most wants to give is the supreme Gift poured out in that hour. He wants you to obtain for us this gift especially. He wants us to ask for this gift above all others. In pointing you to his hour, Jesus already seems to be saying what he will say later to the woman at the well, "If you knew the gift of God, and who it is who is saying to you, 'Give me a drink,' you would have asked him and he would have given you living water" (John 4:10). "Now he said this of the Holy Spirit, which those who believed in him were to receive; for as yet the Spirit had not been given, because Jesus was not yet glorified" (John 7:39).

But in directing our attention to this gift, "the living water," Jesus does not intend to refuse us the other things we will ask also. "If you ask *anything* in my name, I will do it" (John 14:14). That is why he did grant your lesser request at Cana, Mary, but only after referring you to his hour, putting the lesser gift, the wine of Cana, within the context of the supreme Gift, the Holy Spirit. All else that God gives us in answer to our prayers is sign and pledge that even now he is giving us eternal life in the Holy Spirit, fruit of the paschal sacrifice. He does not want us to fail to see this.

And if often he seems to delay answering our other requests, it is perhaps because we have not sufficiently placed our requests within the sacrifice of Jesus, and have not desired most of all the life of the Spirit. When we desire to seek first his Holy Spirit, all else will be given to us besides. "Seek first his kingdom and his righteousness, and all these things shall be yours as well" (Matthew 6:33). "For the kingdom of God does not mean food and drink, but righteousness and peace and joy in the Holy Spirit" (Romans 14:17). The kingdom is communion with God in communion with one another, in the Holy Spirit.

Expectant Hope

Mary, your Son's generosity at Cana surpassed all your expectations. Thus you learned to hope for the gifts which surpass all understanding. Mother, by your maternal influence, form this same hope in us. Whenever we ask for wine, show us how to expect the Holy Spirit (John 2). When we ask for daily bread, teach us to look for the Bread of Life (John 6). When we ask for sight for the blind (John 9), open our eyes to see your Son, who said, "I am the light of the world; he who follows me will not walk in darkness, but will have the light of life" (John 8:12).

When we ask for the healing of a cripple (John 5), obtain for us the strength to walk in the light of life all the way home to our Father's house. When we pray for a house to live in, remind us to seek the home in our Father's house which Jesus has prepared for us by going to the Father by way of the cross (John 14). When we ask for clothing, teach us to desire to be like you, Mother, "clothed with the sun," transformed with the glory of your Son, the risen Lord (Revelation 12:1).

Mary, show us how to expect these marvels even while we ask and receive the lesser gifts from our loving Father. May your persistent faith at Cana inspire us with the faith which God loves best: the faith and hope which expects all the wonderful gifts of the Holy Spirit which he wants to pour out upon us.

14

MARY, THE FIRST BELIEVER
IN THE LORD

Unless You See Signs and Wonders

Throughout John's Gospel, Jesus always seems reluctant to work miracles (John 4:48; 2:18). He is saddened that his miracles are so often misunderstood (John 6:26; 2:23-25). People are so attracted by the marvelous aspect of these works that they fail to look beyond to their deeper meaning. Therefore Jesus persistently takes care to call attention to this deeper meaning.

He does this, for example, before the two signs he works at Cana. In the literary structure of John's Gospel, these two events are parallel, and therefore the two signs are to be interpreted in the light of each other. We can fully grasp the significance of the miracle of the wine at Cana (John 2:1-11) only if we reflect on it in connection with the healing of the royal official's son on the Lord's next visit to Cana (John 4:46-54).

The Lord's remark to the official on that occasion is very helpful in enabling us to grasp what he means at Cana when he says to you, Mary, "Woman, what is that to me and to you? My hour has not yet come."

He says to the official, "Unless you *see* signs and wonders, you will not believe" (John 4:48). Jesus wants people to believe in his *word,* whether they see miracles or not. What he says to the official is already a preparation for one of his last remarks in John's Gospel, "Blessed are those who have *not seen,* and yet believe" (John 20:29).

The official repeats his request even more urgently, "Sir, come down before my son dies!" (John 4:49). Jesus says to him, "Go, your son will live!" The evangelist then says, "The man believed *the word* that Jesus spoke to him, and went his way" (John 4:50). The man does not have to see a miracle in order to believe. He accepts the Lord's word.

As he goes home, his servants meet him and tell him that his son is living. When he asks them at what hour he became well, they tell him, "Yesterday at the seventh hour." The father knows that is the hour in which Jesus had said to him, "Your son will live." And the father *believes,* and all his household.

What does the father believe this time? Before his son's cure, he believed the Lord's *word.* But the word was fulfilled when the son was cured. What does the father now believe?

The answer to this is contained in John's account of the first sign Jesus worked at Cana. The cure of the official's son is the second sign, and it is to be interpreted in the light of the first one, the miracle of the wine. "This, the first of his signs, Jesus did at Cana in Galilee, and *manifested his glory,* and his disciples believed *in him"* (John 2:11).

So too the official and his household *see his glory* manifested in a sign, and they believe *in the Lord,* for the Lord is the deeper reality manifested in these signs. The signs manifest his glory as Son of God and giver of God's life to men. "Your son will *live,"* Jesus says to the official, and he believes this word. Now he believes in Jesus as *Life!*

What Jesus wants from the official, and from all of us, is this true faith which does not look for signs and wonders, but penetrates through the signs directly to his own glory as Son of God and giver of life. He never wants people to set their hearts on miracles as though these wonderful works were the whole purpose of his coming. His miracles are only signs pointing to the magnificent work of life which he can accomplish only in those who believe *in him* and surrender themselves to him.

Mary, First Believer in the Lord

The Lord himself brings you, Mary, to this deeper faith by addressing to you a remark similar to the words he will later address to the official. To the official he will say, "Unless you see signs and wonders, you will not believe." To you he says, "Woman, what is that to me and to you? My hour has not yet come."

In either remark, his purpose is the same. Before working the miracle which you request, he wants to be sure that you will not stop at the miracle as though that were all he had to give you. He points beyond the miracle to his hour. He wants us to realize that his miracles are only signs pointing to the hour of his crucifixion and resurrection, in which we see his glory as Son of God who gives the Holy Spirit.

Mary, even though at Cana you do not yet realize the full meaning of his hour, you do get the point that he wants you to look beyond your request, and to expect more than miraculous wine. And, like the official, you believe even before you see the miracle, and you go about having the servants make preparations for it. You believe in him as Messiah, one who is infinitely more than a mere worker of wonders which satisfy only earthly needs.

Later on, at the feeding of five thousand with five loaves, the crowds will fail to get this point, and Jesus will have to chide them for seeking only food which perishes, rather than the Bread which endures to eternal life (John 6:27). But after his words to you at Cana, you believe in the greater realities which he has to offer. Thus you are the first of his disciples to understand in faith that there is a deeper reality beyond the miracles. And you are the first one to ask for this reality with enlightened faith.

Mother of Faith

When you turn to the servants to enlist their help in preparing for the miracle of the wine, you are indeed persevering in your original request for the wine, but you are not persisting without due reflection. Rather, you have pondered your Son's reference to his hour, and his seeming refusal of your request. In this pondering, your faith has been enlightened, and you no longer seek the wine merely for its own sake. You want it now as a sign of the marvelous realities which all of us are to expect from the Lord.

Not only do you yourself now believe on this deeper level, expecting the reality which is behind the sign, but you invite the servants to the same faith. The servants are symbols of all would-be disciples of the Lord. You invite them to believe his word and obey his will, whatever it may be:

> "Do whatever he tells you" (John 2:5). He has greater things in store for you than you could ever dream of asking for! Believe in his word and act upon it, entrusting yourself totally to him.

Thus you prepare the hearts of the disciples for faith by preparing for the sign in which your son will manifest his glory and will win their faith. "This first of his signs Jesus did at Cana in Galilee and manifested his glory, and his disciples believed in him" (John 2:11).

What counts is not the miracle, but the person of Jesus, and total surrender to him in faith, with obedience to his word, that he might accomplish in us the greater wonders of which his miracles are only the sign.

Thus your faith at Cana precedes and surpasses the faith of the disciples. In preparing the disciples for faith, you are the mother of the faith of the community of the Lord's first disciples, the community which becomes the Christian Church. You are Mother of the Church. You are mother of faith in all of us.

By your faith at Cana, you are the Church before anyone else. You are a corporate personality in whom the Church's faith is already operative. This is true of your faith at the Annunciation, for there too Luke presents you as the representative of the whole people of God.

Such perceptive faith is possible for you at Cana because your Son has long been preparing you for it, through your pondering of all the words concerning him, and all the words which he himself spoke (Luke 2:19,33,51). His glory could not have failed to shine through to you in some measure even before Cana, for he had spoken to you even in his childhood about his Father's house (Luke 2:49).

Lord, Trust Yourself to Us!

I have to ponder the incidents at Cana in the context of John's whole Gospel if I wish to grasp their full significance, and come to understand your role in my life as Mother of Faith. The Lord's remark to you, "My hour has not yet come," is only the beginning of his persistence throughout the Gospel of John in trying to bring all of us to a deeper penetration of his role as Son of God and giver of the Spirit. In practically every discourse in John's Gospel, people interpret the Lord's miracles and understand his words on too shallow a level. He must therefore patiently lead them to the deeper levels.

The woman at the well, for example, thinks Jesus is talking about natural water (John 4:11). He leads her to know "the living water welling up to eternal life" (John 4:10,14). The crowds at Capernaum are looking for bread to feed their bodies (John 6:26). Jesus leads them to himself as the living bread come down from heaven. The people he meets on his mission are looking only for marvelous miracles. He draws their attention to himself as the bread of life, the light of the world, the resurrection and the life, the true vine, the way, the truth, and the life.

He cannot trust himself to them as long as they are seeking only signs and wonders, or the merely material things they expect him to give in his miracles. John tells us this when he writes, "Many believed in his name, but Jesus did not trust himself to them, because he knew all men" (John 2:23-25). He cannot trust himself to them as Indwelling Guest (John 14:23), for he knows that their hearts are set on the merely miraculous and on the earthly, and that therefore they are not open and surrendered to him. He cannot be their bread of life or their living waters, he cannot come to them and make his home in them (John 14:23), until their faith has been enlightened like yours at Cana, and their believing is expressed in a surrender of self to him.

You exercise your influence as mother of our faith by preparing our hearts for the enlightened faith which penetrates to the interior of the divine mystery. Already at the Annunciation Jesus can trust himself totally to you, because you believe and obey the word of God brought to you by the angel. Because of your enlightened faith and obedient surrender, Jesus comes to you and makes his home in your heart and in your womb. You know him as no one else does. Help us to know who he is, and what he is for us—Son of God, true light, living bread, resurrection and life, way and truth and life, and Indwelling Guest.

O Mary, these are the interior wonders you want us to expect from your Son, rather than striking external miracles, or merely earthly gifts. You want us to receive him as our living bread, you want him to dwell in our hearts. You want your Son to entrust himself totally to us. These are the graces you desire to obtain for us as you continue the intercession you began at Cana.

Your role as spiritual mother is to bring us to Jesus, so that in the fullness of faith we will entrust ourselves totally to him, saying like Thomas, "My Lord and my God!" (John 20:28). Then we will hear the Lord's words of approval:

> "Blessed are you who have not seen and yet believe!" (John 20:29). Blessed are you who have entered into the interior of my mystery, and dwell in me because I dwell in you. "We will come to him and make our home with him" (John 14:23).

O Mother Mary, form faith like this in my heart, so that Jesus can trust himself totally to me!

John, True Son of Mary

Mother, John the Evangelist tells us that it was only after the Lord's resurrection that the disciples came to the full understanding of what he said and did (John 2:22; 12:16). John was among those disciples who believed in Jesus when he manifested his glory at Cana, and it is John who shows you to us preparing the hearts of the disciples for this faith. But the Lord's glory at Cana was but a pre-figuring of his glory in the resurrection. Was John imply-ing in the Cana story that you prepared the hearts of the disciples for belief in his resurrection as well?

Was it your maternal influence over John which pre-pared him to be the first disciple to believe in the resur-rection? John recognized the risen Lord even before Peter did. When he entered the tomb after Peter, and saw the napkin and the linen cloths, he believed immediately, though he does not say that Peter believed immediately (John 20:8). Mary Magdalene was still looking for a stolen corpse after John had gone home believing (John 20:9-10). Later, when the risen Lord appeared standing on the shore of the lake, again John was the one who recognized him first, and said to Peter, "It is the Lord!" (John 21:7).

How did it happen that John was the first to recog-nize the risen Lord, the first to penetrate profoundly into his mystery, the one who has brought us more deeply into it than any of the other evangelists?

Was it not because he was with you, Mary, at the foot of the cross? Was it not because Jesus entrusted him to you as the first of your spiritual sons? Was it not be-cause you opened his heart to the light?

Is not this why John can present you to us in the scene at Cana with such conviction as the one who prepares the hearts of the disciples for faith in your Son? Is not John sharing with all of us what he himself had experienced in the hour of the Lord's death and resurrection?

Certainly this was the opinion of that ancient writer who said, "The flower of all the Sacred Scriptures is the Gospels, and the flower of the Gospels is the Gospel written by John, whose meaning no one can penetrate unless he too has reposed upon Christ's breast, and from Jesus has received Mary as his mother" (Origen).

And St. Ambrose writes, "It is not surprising that John, better than any other, has dealt with the divine mysteries, for he, more than any other, was close to Mary."

John, lead us to our mother Mary, so that she can lead us in the power of the Holy Spirit ever more profoundly into the mystery which you present to us in your Gospel: the mystery of God's Son who dwells in us if we dwell in him (John 14:23), and manifests himself to us by his very presence within us (John 14:21-23).

PART III

MARY IN THE TIMELESS MYSTERY OF JESUS

15

THE SLAIN LAMB

Mother, even though the sufferings of your Son nailed to the cross, and your sufferings with him at the foot of the cross, took place at a definite time in history, there is something timeless and eternal about them.

John vividly presents this fact to us in the striking imagery of the Book of Revelation. He depicts your Son as "a Lamb standing as if slain"—risen from death, yet forever bearing in his body the glorious wounds of his crucifixion (Revelation 5:6). In a mysterious and very real way, the sufferings of the risen Lord remain ever present in human history. They are a living source of life and strength for all of us as we "share his sufferings, becoming like him in death, that if possible we may attain the resurrection from the dead" (Philippians 3:10).

In all of us, his members, his own sufferings are present and continued, for he lives in us, and in us he suffers and dies again. "For if we (who have been baptized into Christ) have been united with him in a death like his, we shall certainly be united with him in a resurrection like his" (Romans 6:3,5).

And just as Jesus is forever "the Lamb standing as if slain," so you, Mary, are forever "the woman clothed with the sun," and yet at the same time "with child, crying out in birth pangs, in anguish for delivery" (Revelation 12:1-2). You are clothed with the sun, that is, transformed with the glory of the risen Lord given to you in your Assumption, and yet at the same time you are mysteriously involved in the anguish of Mother Church as she brings forth her children in Christ.

Just as the Lord's sufferings are somehow forever present in his glory, so your sharing in his sufferings is somehow forever contained in your sharing in his glory. For when you stood at the cross of Jesus, you represented in your person the whole people of God, doing on their behalf what all of them must do in turn in their own persons: "carrying in the body the dying of Jesus, so that the life of Jesus may also be manifested in our bodies" (2 Corinthians 4:10).

For in your person at the cross, Mary, Mother Church was already beginning her mission of bringing life to others through her own sharing in the passion of Jesus. Mother Church was somehow in you, beginning in your person her work of continuing the Lord's work of forming his own life in all his members. St. Paul's words concerning his own sufferings, "death is at work in us, but life in you" (2 Corinthians 4:12), are even more fully true of your sufferings with Jesus on Calvary.

Thus, in a mysterious and real way, Mother, the sufferings of Jesus, and your sufferings with him, are ever present with the sufferings of Mother Church. Our sufferings with the Lord are in unbroken continuity with his and yours, as Mother Church continues in us her travail of bringing to birth in Christ all the children of God. For Jesus and you, and all the saints, and we his people on earth, live in the perfect continuity of his Body, which is the Church and the communion of saints. The Church is one glorious Body of Christ along with the saints in heaven, at the same time that she is a mother on earth in the pains of giving birth to God's children. But the whole Body, saints in heaven and faithful on earth, are as one in this work of bringing forth God's children. Christ's Body is one.

Therefore just as Jesus remains forever present with us as the crucified and risen Lord, standing though slain, so the sufferings and the glory of all his saints in heaven are forever present with us as one with his. In the Mystical Body of the risen Lord, there is a continuity of the life and the sufferings of all who, throughout the ages, suffer with Christ and come to glory in him. The sufferings of all the saints who have been taken up into the Lord's own glory continue to influence and to support those members of the Lord's Body who are still in the way of sufferings and being prepared for this glory. The Lord's whole Body, the communion of saints, has a timeless presence to all of us.

What is true of the whole Church in heaven—standing like the Lamb as if slain, clothed with the sun and yet in the pains of giving birth—is true most perfectly in you, Mother Mary, for in you first of all the Lord's paschal mystery has been brought to fulfillment. You stood at his cross on Calvary, and were taken into the fullness of his glory in your assumption into heaven. There you are clothed with the sun, transfigured with the glory of God and of the Lamb. But though you are in glory, both your sufferings and your glory continue to influence all of us in a powerful way as you exercise in the Spirit your maternity in our regard.

That is why I can ask you to be with me as I pray your Rosary, Mother. I ask you to form the life of Jesus in me, as I ponder with you the mysteries of his life. I ask you to help me live all that St. Paul lived so strikingly, and expressed so vividly in these words:

> All I want is to know Christ
> and to experience the power of his resurrection;
> to share in his sufferings and become like him
> in his death, in the hope that I myself will be
> raised from death to life (Phil. 3:10-11).

16

MARY AND THE SERVANT CHURCH

"Mary said to Gabriel, 'I am the servant of the Lord. Let it be done to me as you say' " (Luke 1:38).

Mother Mary, in recording these words of yours, St. Luke is presenting you to us as type of *the Church as Servant of the Lord.* For in the Acts of the Apostles, the continuation of his Gospel, Luke describes the Church as Servant. He shows how her life is a continuation and completion of the life of Jesus, the Servant. The Lord Jesus is living his own life in the Church, and carrying on his work through her. Luke shows, throughout Acts, that there is an identification of the Church with Christ.

In the fourth chapter, for example, the Christian community sees that the attacks against it are a prolongation of the attack upon Jesus himself. Gathered together when Peter and John are released from prison, the faithful quote the second psalm: "Why did the Gentiles rage against the Lord and against his Anointed" (Psalm 2). They see that this psalm is being fulfilled in the sufferings of Jesus and in those of his followers: "Truly, in this city, Herod and Pontius Pilate, with the Gentiles and the peoples of Israel, were gathered together against your holy *Servant Jesus,* whom you annointed" (Acts 4:27). Experiencing this same attack against themselves, they identify themselves with the Servant Jesus in his preaching, and pray for courage to speak his word: "Lord, look upon

111

their threats, and grant to your *servants* to speak your word with all boldness" (Acts 4:29).

On different occasions in Acts, the preachers of the Church are called before the same tribunal which had condemned Jesus to death (Acts 4:5; 5:27; 6:12; 22:30). They face the same charges that Jesus faced. They take the same attitude that Jesus took, and make the same declarations. They are living the Lord's own life and are continuing his own experience.

All this is especially clear in the case of Stephen. Luke shows beautifully how Stephen's martyrdom is a continuation of the Lord's own passion and death. Stephen faces the same Sanhedrin which had condemned Jesus (Acts 6:12; Matthew 26:59). He is accused of the same determination to destroy the temple and the law (Acts 6:13; Matthew 26:59-61). Like Jesus, Stephen warns his judges of the coming of the Son of Man in glory to judge them (Acts 7:56; Matthew 26:64).

As Stephen says this, his judges "saw that his face was like the face of an angel" (Acts 6:15), for the glory of God shone upon it. "Full of the Holy Spirit, Stephen gazed into heaven and saw the glory of God and Jesus standing at the right hand of God" (Acts 7:55). Every Christian as he grows in grace is transfigured with the Lord's glory (2 Corinthians 3:18) like Stephen, and becomes "an angel" of the Lord (Acts 6:15), an image of God, a revelation of God's presence; for God dwells in him.

More strikingly still, Stephen's interior attitudes are identical with those of Jesus. Jesus says, as they nail him to the cross, "Father, forgive them, for they know not what they do" (Luke 23:34). Stephen, as he dies, cries out with a loud voice, 'Lord, do not hold this sin against them" (Acts 7:60). "Jesus, crying out with a loud voice, said, 'Father, into your hands I commit my spirit' " (Luke 23:46). "As they were stoning Stephen, he prayed, 'Lord Jesus, receive my spirit' " (Luke 7:59).

Clearly, the Lord relives his own paschal mystery in his disciples. The glory of God shines forth in his disciples' love.

St. Paul, too, according to Acts, was so conscious of his personal identity with the Lord, the Servant of Yahweh, that he actually applied to himself and to Barnabas the description of the Suffering Servant given by Isaiah (Acts 13:47; Isaiah 49:6). Yet Paul knew full well that from the beginning the Church had interpreted the Servant Poems as referring to Jesus. Paul sees himself in these poems because the Lord, using the words of the poem, has said to him, "I have made you a light to the nations, a means of salvation to the ends of the earth" (Isaiah 49:6; Acts 13:47). The Lord spoke the same words to all his disciples as he ascended into heaven: "You are my witnesses . . . even to the ends of the earth" (Acts 1:8; Isaiah 43:10; 49:6).

All the Servant Poems in Isaiah refer to Jesus. By describing his apostles in these same words, the Lord identifies himself with his missionaries. Paul knows that the accomplishment of the Servant's work among the nations is entrusted to him, and in the measure that he is the Lord's representative, the texts of Isaiah refer to him as well as to Jesus. Therefore they refer also to the whole Church in its mission to the nations.

Repeatedly in his letters Paul refers to himself in words echoing the Servant Poems. He does this especially when he speaks of his own sufferings as being fruitful for the salvation of others (2 Corinthians 4:12), because they fill up what is wanting to the sufferings of Christ for his body, the Church (Colossians 1:24).

In Acts, Luke describes Paul's last journey to Jerusalem in words which strikingly parallel his description of the Lord's own journey to Jerusalem to die. In his Gospel, Luke tells how the Lord steadfastly set his face to go up to Jerusalem (Luke 9:51), and said, along the way, that the Son of Man "will be delivered up to the Gentiles" (Luke 18:32). When the Lord is arrested and stands before Pilate, the crowds cry out, 'Away with this man!" (Luke 23:18).

Luke echoes all these words when he speaks of Paul's journey to Jerusalem. At Caesarea, the prophet Agabus foretells that Paul will be bound in chains if he goes up to Jerusalem, and "the Jews will deliver him into the hands of the Gentiles" (Acts 21:11). Though the people beg Paul not to go up, like the Lord himself Paul steadfastly sets out, saying, "I am ready not only to be imprisoned, but even to die at Jerusalem for the name of the Lord Jesus" (Acts 21:13). When he is arrested at Jerusalem, the crowds cry out against him in the same words they had used against Jesus, "Away with this man!" (Acts 21:36; Luke 23:18). Paul, like Jesus and Stephen, is accused of destroying the temple (Acts 21:28), and is brought before the same body which had condemned Jesus and Stephen (Acts 23:1; 22:30).

Clearly, Luke and Paul are very conscious that the disciples of Jesus continue their Lord's own journey of preaching, suffering, and death.

Mother Mary, what does all this have to do with you? It certainly helps us to understand the meaning of your presence at the cross of Jesus. If the labors and sufferings and martyrdom of Paul and the other apostles are a sharing in the paschal mystery of the Suffering Servant, and are fruitful for the salvation of their fellowmen, what can we say about your total participation in that mystery as you stood at the cross?

If Luke, who knew you so well, presents you at the beginning of his Gospel as Servant of the Lord and type of the Servant Church, surely he must have more to say about your personal sharing in the Lord's sufferings. Why then in his story of the passion of Jesus does he fail to mention your presence on Calvary? Why did he wait for John to give us the picture of you standing at the cross? Was it not because he chose to give, in his story of the Presentation, an even more striking picture than John's of your sharing in the Lord's sufferings?

17

THE TIMELESS PRESENTATION

Mary, there is something timeless about the mystery of the Presentation of the Lord (Luke 2:22-40), for it is one with the mystery of the Lamb standing as if slain. Indeed, Revelation refers to him as "the Lamb who has been slain from the foundation of the world" (Revelation 13:8). It was eternally decreed by the Father that Jesus should come into the world to be the true Paschal Lamb. It was he who would take away the sins of the world through the paschal sacrifice in which he would offer himself.

Mary, how much of this did you realize when you brought the infant Jesus to the temple to consecrate him to the Lord? That consecration was a foreshadowing of his consecration on the cross.

Simeon certainly gave you much to ponder when he indicated to you that Jesus would be the Suffering Servant (Luke 2:32; Isaiah 42:6). Mother, when you called yourself "Servant of the Lord" at the Annunciation (Luke 1:38), and again at the Visitation (Luke 1:48), did you realize to what extent you would be involved with the Suffering Servant on Calvary?

Nowhere in the Scriptures is your total involvement in the Lord's passion more fully pictured than in Luke's story of the Lord's Presentation (Luke 2:22-40). Simeon's words to you on that occasion are the key to our understanding of you as a suffering servant with Jesus: "Behold this child is set for the fall and rising of many in Israel, and for a sign that is spoken against — and a sword shall pierce through your own soul also" (Luke 2:34).

Luke's story of the Lord's infancy (Luke 1 - 2) builds up to a climax in this scene. He presents the whole story as the Child's journey, in your womb and then in your arms, up to the temple, where he is presented to the Lord. But this journey and its climax is symbolic of the Lord's whole life as a journey up to Jerusalem, where his life is presented to God on the cross. His Body, his people, becomes the new living temple when he pours out the Holy Spirit upon them as the fruit of his sacrifice.

Mary, your journeying *with him* in his infancy and childhood is symbolic of your participation in his journey to the Father by way of the cross. And since you are type of the Church, it reveals our sharing in the cross as well.

To the extent that anyone of us enters into the Lord and his paschal mystery, we are his Body, in which and through which he continues his redeeming work in the world. To the extent that the paschal mystery is perfected in any member of the Lord, and that person is transformed in the Lord, the person's life is fruitful in the Lord for others. This is the principle which Paul experienced at work in his own life: "while we live we are always being given up to death for Jesus' sake, so that the life of Jesus may be manifested in our mortal flesh. So death is at work in us, but life in you" (2 Corinthians 4:11).

Mother Mary, Jesus completed his paschal mystery in you first of all, as you stood at his cross sharing fully in his dying, so that he could bring you into the glory of his own resurrection by assuming you into heaven. If St. Paul teaches that his personal involvement in the sufferings of Jesus is so fruitful for the salvation of those to whom he preaches, who will dare to say, Mary, that your involvement with Jesus at the cross is not fruitful in the Lord for the salvation of all of us? To deny such value to your union with Jesus Crucified is to deny all value to the sufferings of any Christian with Christ. It is to deny all identity of the Christian with the suffering Lord, even though Paul many times explicitly asserts this identity. "I rejoice in my sufferings for your sake, and in my flesh I complete what is lacking in Christ's afflictions for the sake of his body, that is, the Church" (Colossians 1:24).

The Living Temple

Mother, you were never hailed before the Sanhedrin and accused of destroying the temple, as Jesus and Stephen and Paul were. But you were fully involved in the mystery of the building of the new temple, "the temple of his body," the Church (John 2:21). It is probably no coincidence that John speaks of this new temple immediately after his story of the mystery of Cana, which foreshadows your participation in the hour of the cross (John 2:13-22).

In Luke's Gospel, your Son's journey in your arms to be presented to the Lord in the temple prefigures his paschal journey on the cross, in which you too are involved. But the journey on the cross does not end in the earthly temple in Jerusalem, as the infancy journey did. It ends in the living temple, God's people. For in the Acts, Luke shows the outcome of the Lord's journey home to his Father. From the Father, Jesus receives the promised Holy Spirit (Acts 2:33), and pours him out upon his people. Thenceforth they are the temple in which God dwells (Revelation 21:3; Ephesians 2:21).

The timeless mystery of the Presentation, then, is one with the mystery of "the Lamb standing as if slain" (Revelation 5:6). Now that the mystery of the Presentation is fulfilled in the Lord's death and resurrection, all the grace of the Presentation is available to us in the power of the risen Lord. This grace of the Holy Spirit fashions in us a sharing in the passion like your own, Mother. And in these sufferings, the living temple is being built. We are being polished as living stones which will fit perfectly into the finished structure (1 Peter 2:4).

O Mother, obtain for me these fruits of the passion! By your maternal influence in my life, the fruit of your own sharing in the Lord's sufferings, strengthen me to desire sincerely, with all my heart, what Paul desired so ardently: "that I may know Christ, and the power of his resurrection, and may share his sufferings, becoming like him in death, that if possible I may attain the resurrection from the dead" (Philippians 3:10).

"This child is set for the fall and rising of many in Israel" (Luke 2:34). Mother, may I rise from death with him!

18

JESUS SCORNED

Mary, I look at Fra Angelico's painting showing your Son mocked and buffeted and spit upon, and I see you in the picture, pondering these things in your heart. The Scriptures nowhere record that you were in the praetorium looking on during your Son's scourging and mockery and crowning with thorns. And yet Angelico is completely accurate in showing us that you lived these events in your heart at the very time they were taking place in reality. For during the preceding years Jesus had carefully attuned you to the mystery of his coming sufferings.

He began this process of leading you into the heart of his paschal mystery when he was twelve years old. He continued the process at Cana. And if we ponder carefully all the other words in the Scriptures which Jesus addressed directly to you or spoke in your presence, we see that each of these words brought you into a deeper understanding of his sufferings and their purpose. Each time Jesus spoke, as listening mother you had to revise somewhat your understanding of him and his work, and of how you were to share in his work. And your loving response and acceptance on each occasion brought you into ever deeper participation in the paschal mystery.

The prophecy of Simeon, "a sword will pierce through your own soul" (Luke 2:35), had already oriented your pondering in the direction of the cross, and had prepared your heart to receive the sword of your Son's word each time he would address it to you. God's word is always like a two-edged sword, piercing our hearts and separating us from preconceived thoughts and intentions, giving us new thoughts and directions (Hebrews 4:12; Luke 2:35).

Your twelve-year-old Son's words to you when you found him in the temple were already saying to you, "My thoughts are not your thoughts, neither are my ways your ways, says the Lord" (Isaiah 55:8). Your gentle rebuke of Jesus, "Son, why have you treated us so? Behold, your father and I have been looking for you anxiously" (Luke 2:48), wins a gentle rebuke in return, "Why were you looking for me? Did you not know that I must be in my Father's house?" (Luke 2:49).

Jesus is telling you that his Father's will is the determining factor in his life, and he must follow it, no matter how painful it is to him and to you. The Father's will has always been the determining factor in your life, too. Luke shows us how you surrendered to his will wholeheartedly at the Annunciation, and how you were ever pondering his word, seeking his will, studying his plan.

But no matter how faithful we are in seeking his will, his ways are always infinitely above our comprehension. Therefore at every new turn in our lives, he has to intervene personally, to turn our thoughts and intentions into unsuspected new directions in which he is leading us. "For as the heavens are higher than the earth, so are my ways higher than your ways, and my thoughts than your thoughts" (Isaiah 55:9). Jesus' simple words to you at the finding in the temple are a foreshadowing of many more words like this which he will address to you in the years to come, each time leading you more deeply into the mystery of his sufferings.

Who Is My Mother?

There was the occasion when the relatives of Jesus set out to seize him, because, they said, "He is out of his mind" (Mark 3:21). They must put an end to the insanity of his preaching! It is likely that you came with them, Mary, not because you were opposed to him or in doubt about him as they seemed to be, but because you were concerned for his safety.

When you arrived with them, the crowds sitting about Jesus said to him, "Your mother and your brothers are outside, asking for you." And he replied, "Who are my mother and my brothers?" And looking around on those who sat about him, he said, "Here are my mother and my brothers! Whoever does the will of God is my brother, and sister, and mother" (Mark 3:31-35).

On this occasion, Mary, you see the prophecy of Simeon in process of being fulfilled: "Behold, this child is set for the fall and rising of many in Israel, and for a sign that is spoken against; and a sword will pierce through your own soul also" (Luke 2:34). Your heart is pierced with sorrow when you see that he is rejected even by some of his closest relatives, who are your own flesh and blood. "He came to his own home, and his own people received him not" (John 1:11).

Seeing this rejection, you become more accurately attuned than before to the mystery of your Son's sufferings. Even now you have already become involved in these sufferings through your faith and acceptance of the One who is being rejected. "But to all who received him, who believed in his name," as you did, "he gave power to become children of God" (John 1:12). These are the ones who are his true brothers and sisters and mother, for they do the will of the Father in accepting the Son.

Your acceptance of the Father's will as you stood at the cross expanded your motherhood far beyond its original limits. From your Son's words, "Whoever does the will of God is my brother and sister and mother," you had learned that he came to give divine life to all who do God's will. These become his brothers and sisters through a sharing in his own divine sonship. You came to understand how your motherhood of Jesus was to expand to include all these brothers and sisters of Jesus.

For the life he came to bring breaks out of the narrow limits of flesh and blood relationships into a communion of all men in God's own life. Your motherly love could no longer be limited only to Jesus himself as your flesh and blood. It had to reach out to embrace all those whom he redeemed by shedding the blood you gave him. Therefore your maternity broke through the limits of your flesh and blood relationship with Jesus and reached out to embrace all the disciples of Jesus.

Universal love like this, transcending all restrictions of blood relationship, is the mark of God's children. "If you salute only your brethren, what more are you doing than others? Do not even the Gentiles do the same? You therefore must be perfect, as your heavenly Father is perfect" (Matthew 5:47). Mary, your love for your Son, like all authentic love for the Lord, reaches out to embrace all those for whom he died, and thus is truly universal.

Pondering Jesus Scorned

Since you were always pondering God's will, Mary, Fra Angelico was right in showing you pondering the sufferings of Jesus while they were in progress, and searching out God's will expressed in these word-events. But were you aware of the details of what was happening when

Jesus was being scourged and crowned with thorns? Had the news reached you that he had been arrested?

Certainly at least one of the scattered disciples must have run to you to tell you what had happened in Gethsemane. Was it that young man who ran naked from the garden? (Mark 14:52). Tradition loves to think that this youngster was John Mark, the man who later wrote Mark's Gospel. Perhaps even then his mother's house in Jerusalem was open to the disciples of Jesus, as it certainly was after Pentecost (Acts 12:12). Mary, were you a guest in that home the night of Jesus' arrest? If the young man ran straight home, then you received news of Jesus' arrest very quickly.

Perhaps you needed no human messenger to bring you this news. How often the Holy Spirit moves one of us to pray for a friend in need, and later we find out that this person was indeed in need at the time we were moved to pray. Surely, Mary, filled with the Holy Spirit, you must have been moved by the Spirit to pray for Jesus that night when he was in agony in the garden and was in need of strength from heaven. As delicately tuned to your Son as you were, you must have been present with him in the Holy Spirit that night, suffering with him.

You must have spent the rest of that night in prayer, struggling with the Father's will in the same way that Jesus struggled with it in the garden. Fra Angelico is not mistaken in showing you deeply moved and involved in the Lord's sufferings throughout that night. And the outcome of the struggle in your case was identical with the outcome in your Son's case. For Jesus had carefully attuned you ever more accurately to the Father's ways. In each of the successive words he had addressed to you or spoke in your presence—at the finding in the temple, at Cana, on the occasion we have just discussed, in the pre-

dictions of his passion — he gave you something new to ponder, so that you were ever revising your understanding of him, and coming to a clearer grasp of God's thoughts and purposes in his regard and yours. And you were always responsive to the Father, just as you were at the Annunciation.

Through your acceptance of the Father's will in consenting to your Son's death, your motherhood had broken through the limits of blood relationship to embrace as your children all those for whom Jesus died. Jesus indicated this fact to you when he said to you from the cross, "Behold your son." John, standing at the cross, was symbol of all those who became your children through your acceptance of the Father's will that you give up your Son Jesus. "Behold your mother!" You are my mother!

Pondering His Death and Resurrection

How astounding was the way in which Jesus fulfilled all the expectations of his people Israel when he reigned as King nailed hands and feet to a cross! Mary, in telling you about the Son you would conceive, Gabriel had declared, "The Lord will give to him the throne of his father David, and he will reign over the house of Jacob forever" (Luke 1:32). Mary, did it occur to you then that one day you would see him exalted on a cross, reigning as the crucified One, with these words written over his head, "Jesus of Nazareth, the king of the Jews" (John 19:19)?

When Jesus spoke of himself as a crucified King, how preposterous the people thought this was! " 'And I, when I am lifted up from the earth, will draw all men to myself.' He said this to show by what death he was to die. The crowd answered him, 'We have heard from the law that the Christ remains forever. How can you says that the Son of Man must be lifted up?' " (John 12:32).

How strange and paradoxical was the way in which Jesus fulfilled every word of God! In his dying moment, "knowing that all was now finished," that all the Scriptures were fulfilled, "he said, 'It is finished!' And he bowed his head and gave up his spirit" (John 19:28).

Mary, what faith it took on your part to adhere with all your heart to this unbelievable fulfillment of the Scriptures! "Who would believe what we have heard!" says Isaiah (53:1), speaking of the Suffering Servant who will astonish kings and nations (Isaiah 52:13).

Your heart never wavered in faith, Mother, for you had always been faithful in listening to the word, seeking to penetrate its true meaning. Each time Jesus had spoken to you, he gave you something new to ponder, forcing you to revise your ideas about him and how he would accomplish his work. Your pondering and your growth in understanding was not completed till Jesus said from the cross, "It is finished!" For only in the light of that fulfillment could all that Israel had pondered through the centuries be understood at last.

Faithful Israel

Only by pondering the events of the cross and the resurrection could you at last come to a full understanding of all that you had pondered through the years since your Son's conception in your womb.

As you stood at the cross, and as you saw your Son dead and buried, you revised once again all your thinking about him—and the thinking of all your people Israel! Was it not in your pondering heart that Israel at last came to the full understanding of the Messiah? Is not this part of what Luke is telling us in presenting you in his infancy gospel as Daughter Israel, in whose person all of Israel's faith and expectant hope at last reaches fulfillment? The old liturgy for the Feast of the Immaculate Conception was not mistaken when it addressed you, saying, "You are the glory of Jerusalem, the surpassing joy of Israel; you are the splendid boast of our people" (Judith 15:9). In your person, Israel remains faithful, never falling away from her Lord, and coming to an ever deeper understanding of him. You are the type of the faithful Church, which, filled with the Holy Spirit and unwavering faith, can never fall away from the divine Bridegroom, and penetrates ever more profoundly into his mystery.

Just as your faith was unwavering in the darkness of Calvary, so too the light of the risen Lord must have shone first of all in your heart. We can only guess at how much of John's and Luke's wisdom was received from you, Seat of Wisdom, who first came to full enlightenment.

19

THE IKON OF THE MOTHER OF SORROWS

Ikons and the Presence of God

Every art form can be used effectively in conveying God's message. Fra Angelico, of the Order of Preachers, did his best and most enduring preaching through his immortal paintings. Just as the Lord's presence among us is manifest and operative in vocal preaching of the word, so his presence can be manifest and effective through painting and sculpture, architecture and music, song and dance, dramatic arts and liturgical ceremony. That is why the great medieval cathedrals are often called "sermons in stone," and stained glass windows in churches have been called "the Bible of the illiterate."

But it is not just the illiterate who need visual and tangible expressions of the mystery of Christ. Everyone needs these, even the most literate and intellectual, and perhaps they especially, lest their religion be only of the head and not of the heart. In a glance at a work of art, a whole page of the Bible can come alive for a person. A look at a crucifix, or at a painting of Jesus crowned with thorns, or at a nativity scene under a Christmas tree, can be enough to stir up faith in our hearts, bringing a consciousness of the Lord's presence and an experience of his love.

Among all the art forms expressing the good news of God's presence among men, there is something special about the ikons of the Eastern Churches, which are used in close relationship with the divine liturgy.

The word "ikon" derives from the Greek word meaning "image." St. Paul calls Christ, the Beloved Son, "the image of the invisible God" (Col. 1:15). In biblical language, "image" means a presence and manifestation of the one imaged. Because God is transcendently superior to all our human powers of perception, he has chosen to manifest his presence and to reveal his nature in his Beloved Son.

The living Lord Jesus is the primary ikon of God. In the Eastern Churches, the liturgical paintings of the Lord and of his saints are also called ikons, for they are considered manifestations of the presence of God.

There are two characteristics of an ikon which we should note particularly.

First, the painter of an ikon consciously strives to manifest the presence of God. Christ, ikon of God, truly is present with us, for as risen Lord he is present everywhere in the power of his Holy Spirit. The ikon artist strives to manifest that presence so that the viewer of his picture will respond to the presence in faith, hope and love.

Secondly, the artist strives to manifest the mystery in its totality, both in its time-bound and in its eternal aspects. In any one scene from Christ's life, he tries to make present the whole mystery of Christ. For example, in the ikon of the Lord's nativity, the complete mystery of the redemption is depicted and made present. To signify that the Infant in the manger came to die for our sins and to free us from the bonds of death, the Infant's swaddling clothes are depicted as burial wrappings, like those which tightly wrapped the dead body of Jesus as it lay in the tomb. The cave at Bethlehem resembles a tomb in the earth. It calls to mind the underworld into which Jesus descended when he died, and from which he freed Adam and Eve and the patriarchs and prophets, bringing them forth with him in his resurrection.

St. John Chrysostom says, "The Feast of the Nativity already contains in it the Epiphany, Easter, and Pentecost." Any one of the feasts contains all the others, for in every feast we celebrate *the risen Lord,* who eternally contains in his Person the totality of his life on earth so that he might reproduce that life in each one of us in whom he lives.

Ikons and the Communion of Saints

The Lord Jesus has chosen to use his holy ones as co-workers in his own work, and therefore they too are ikons of God. For the Lord wills to be present and manifest to mankind through them. "He who receives you," he said to them, "receives me, and he who receives me, receives him who sent me" (Matthew 10:40). Therefore when we are in communion with the Lord's co-workers, we are in communion with the Lord himself. And when we are in communion with him, we are in communion with his all-holy Father.

But those who work with the Lord during their mission on earth continue to work with him on behalf of their fellowmen even after he has taken them up into the fullness of his own glory. That is why the prophet Jeremiah, for example, could appear to his brothers on earth four centuries after his death. During the days of his prophetic mission on earth, Jeremiah had been a presence of Yahweh among his people in Jerusalem. After his death, he continues to love these people, he prays for them ceaselessly, and is present to them with divine help.

All this is expressed in the Book of Maccabees (2 Macc. 15:12-16). Jeremiah appears in a vision to Judas

Maccabaeus, along with another saint, Onias. Onias introduces Jeremiah to Judas, saying, "This is God's prophet Jeremiah, who loves his brethren and fervently prays for his people and their holy city." Though he has been dead for centuries, Jeremiah is alive, and is still with his people in love. Stretching out his right hand, Jeremiah presents a gold sword to Judas, saying, "Accept this holy sword as a gift from God; with it you shall crush your adversaries."

Thus, even before the time of the Lord's coming to earth as man, God's people had already been experiencing the saints' power of intercession on their behalf, and the presence of the saints coming to their aid.

The saints have the privilege and the joy of working with God in establishing his kingdom. God is present to us through his holy ones in glory as well as through his missionaries and ministers on earth. All of God's people, whether in heaven or on earth, share in the Lord's work of being a presence and manifestation of God, and a living instrument of his saving power. Such is the communion of saints. The very person of a saint is an ikon of God, just as the Lord Jesus is; and an ikon or painting of a saint is a manifestation of the saint and of God.

When I behold an ikon, or any other sacred image, faith springs forth from my heart. In this faith, I am in communion with the Lord, or with his mother, or with any friend of the Lord represented in the image. Thus I am brought into communion with the transcendent God himself.

This is possible because the risen Lord Jesus, image of the unseen God, is ever present to all his creatures. And in him, through his Holy Spirit, his saints too can be present with their fellowmen on earth. For in God's plan, we come into communion with God through our communion with his saints, whether these are his church on earth or his church in glory. In our communion with the apostles and the rest of the Christian community, says St. John, we are in communion with the Father and with his Son: "That which we have seen and heard, we proclaim also to you, so that you may have communion with us; and our communion is with the Father and with his Son Jesus Christ" (1 John 1:3).

The loving faith stirred up in my heart as I behold an ikon does not stop at the picture. It penetrates to the living person who is depicted in it, and through this person, to God himself who is manifested in him.

But an ikon not only helps me into the presence of God and of the person it depicts. It also instructs me, leading my faith into a deeper understanding of the mystery it represents. The artist himself has first deeply contemplated this mystery in prayer, and then shows in the ikon what the Lord has revealed to him in prayer. I am made present to the mystery through the ikon, and become deeply involved in the mystery. In prayer, I respond to the mystery and address the persons whose presence is manifested to me in the ikon.

In the following pages, I address the Mother of Jesus, whose presence is manifested to me in the ikon of the Sorrowful Mother. We must remember that an ikon strives to present the total mystery of Christ, in its timeless and in its time-bound aspects. Though in this particular ikon, Mary is holding the infant Jesus in her arms, that Child has been destined from eternity to be the Man of Sorrows, and Simeon has revealed this truth to Mary. His mother, pointing to the Child, is already pointing out to us the cross on which he is nailed for our redemption. In her heart, she is living that mystery into which she is inviting us. With the aid of the ikon, we are present at the cross and are involved in its mystery.

20

THE IKON OF THE SORROWFUL MOTHER

O Mother of God in the Passion! Through my contemplation of this ikon, I greet you present with me in the mystery of your maternity. Though you are depicted as holding the child Jesus in your arms, the artist is really showing you to me in the mystery of your presence at the foot of the cross. You are represented as exercising your divine motherhood during your Son's passion. For at the cross you are fully mother of Jesus and mother of us.

As I contemplate this ikon, I see the mystery of your presence with Jesus during his crucifixion and your continuing presence with me. I see you looking at me, accepting me as your child in Jesus, drawing me into the mystery of the cross. For from the cross, Jesus said to you, referring to me, "Behold your son" (John 19:26).

In this ikon, you are depicted as "Mother, Guide on the Way." In his sufferings in the paschal mystery, Jesus is the Way (John 14:16). Looking at me, you point to him.

Your baby in the picture is frightened when he sees the angels showing him the whips with which he will be scourged, and presenting his cross to him, and he clings to you, seeking strength and courage. In real life, however, this fear of the cross and his drawing back from suffering took place when the time of his passion came ever nearer (John 12:27). His fear reached its peak in the agony in the garden. Why then does the artist portray your Jesus as experiencing this fear when he is still a child in your arms?

Because this mystery of Jesus is timeless. And because the artist wishes to tell us, Mother, that when you stood at the cross, you truly were precisely a mother, comforting your Son and strengthening him by your presence as only a mother can.

But the artist is saying more than this. He is telling me that just as you mothered the crucified Jesus, you mother me when I share in his sufferings. Your motherhood of Jesus is continued and completed in your maternity towards me.

Just as this mystery of Jesus is timeless, so too is your sharing in the mystery. The mystery of your comforting Jesus in his infancy, and giving him courage as he hangs on the cross, and consoling me when I suffer with him, is one and the same mystery. For the mystery of Jesus is complete only when it is completed in me and in all the other members of Christ. And the mystery of your divine maternity, inseparable from the mystery of Jesus, is completed only when you are my mother, and mother of all my sisters and brothers in Jesus.

Mother, Guide on the Way

Mother in the ikon, even while your child Jesus clings to you to find comfort in his fear of the cross, you look straight at me, and point to him with the very hand to which he is clinging. Your eyes and your gesture are telling me that just as I must share in his sufferings, so I may cling to you for courage while I endure them with him.

Obviously, Mary, devotion to you as Mother of Sorrows, who shows the way of the cross, is far from being an escape from responsibility. In pointing to the suffering Jesus, you are showing me my responsibilities and telling me to assume them. Your eyes and your gesture in the ikon say to me firmly, "Do whatever he tells you" (John 2:5).

How this ikon brings home to me the truth of your Son's humanity, and the reality of his sufferings on the cross! Because you are his human mother, the Son of God is completely human even while he is God. He is as tenderly responsive to you as any child is to his loving mother.

Through this very response to you, he becomes tenderly sensitive to all his fellowmen, and filled with compassion for them in their sufferings. For only association with a loving woman can bring out these tender, responsive qualities in a man.

But this very sensitivity of your Son's whole being, developed in his loving response to you, makes him all the more sensitive to his own sufferings when they come his way. And when they come, though he is now a full grown man, his whole human makeup cries out for comfort and courage. And you are there to give it. "Standing by the cross of Jesus was his mother" (John 19:25).

Mary, though your Son's body, nailed to the cross, cannot cling to you in the way he did as an infant, all the tender affection of his being cries out to you from the cross for support, and you give it. But at the same time, his sensitive heart is deeply pained at seeing your pain.

Even while he courageously endures his torments, truly helped by you, he thinks of me, along with all my suffering fellowmen. And he recommends me to you, saying, "Woman, behold your son!" For he knows that I, too, when I must suffer with him and share in his cross, will be supported and encouraged by you, and strengthened to bear the burdens of my responsibilities.

For it is your mission as mother, just as it is the mission of Mother Church and all the people who are the

Church, to bring forth Christ in others like a mother in the pangs of birth, "filling up what is wanting to the sufferings of Christ for his body, the Church" (Col. 1:24). Mary, standing at the cross, more truly than St. Paul, you can say to all of us, "My little children, with whom I am again in travail until Christ be formed in you" (Gal. 4:19).

How many of God's holy ones have experienced your maternal influence, especially in the darkest night of their sufferings with the Lord! When they were forced to cry out like Jesus, "My God, my God, why have you forsaken me" (Matt. 27:46), you were there supporting them as mother by your mysterious mystical presence, strengthening them to persevere and be faithful to the end.

In the history of the Christian experience of transforming union with Christ, how many bear witness, Mother, to your presence with them as they were undergoing the dark night! In the purifying trials preparing them for mystical union with the Lord, you have the role of mitigating the painfulness of the trials. You do this by softening our resistance to the Lord, fashioning our hearts in the likeness of your own generous "Yes" to him. You give us your own humility and faith, and your generous surrender and faithfulness. Thus we are freed of the pain which comes from resistance to the Lord. We joyfully carry our cross with him. "For my yoke is sweet and my burden is light" (Matt. 11:30).

21

LOVE'S AUTHORITY

Mother, through the ikon of the Sorrowful Mother, you are present with me in the fullness of the mystery of Cana and of Calvary, the paschal mystery which has been completed in Jesus and in you.

When I begin to look at you in the ikon, you are already looking at me, drawing my attention, inviting my love, winning my response. Your whole person is an ikon of God, a presence and revelation of his love. Everything about you, your eyes, your gesture, the tilt of your head, reveal to me God's love and your love. Your love is itself a presence and revelation and communication of God's love.

While your hand points to Jesus, your eyes look straight into my eyes, piercing my heart. Your whole loving person is saying to me, "Do whatever he tells you" (John 2:5). This word pierces my heart, for it is the two-edged sword of God's word (Luke 2:35; Heb. 4:12).

To do whatever he tells you, is to abide in his love. For he says, "If you keep my commandments, you will abide in my love, just as I have kept my Father's commandments and abide in his love" (John 15:10).

When you say to me, "Do whatever he tells you," you speak with authority, the only true authority, love's authority, the love which does the very thing it asks me to do, your love which is saying to me, "Abide in his love just as I abide in his love" (Cf. John 15:10). Mother, you do abide in his love, you have always done so, for you have always kept his commandments.

"Commandment" in the Scriptures, even in the Old Testament, always implies the idea of a word of revelation and instruction coming from God's love, and showing the way of true life, the way of love in response to his love.

Jesus has opened a new way of life. "A new commandment I give you, that you love one another; even as I have loved you, that you love one another" (John 13:34). Receive my love, respond to my love, abide in my love by loving as I have loved. "If you keep my commandments you will abide in my love, just as I have kept my Father's commandments and abide in his love" (John 15-10).

Mother, you are saying all of this to me in your simple loving gesture pointing to Jesus. "Do whatever he tells you. Abide in his love by loving as he loved, just as I, too, have loved as he has loved." Mother, you ask of me only what you have done yourself, and you ask it in the love in which you have done it. You have kept his word, just as he has kept his Father's word. When he pointed you towards his cross by his reference at Cana to his hour, you followed in the way he indicated, and came to stand at his cross.

Thus, there is nothing sentimental about devotion to you as Mother of Sorrows. As I look at you in the Mystery of the cross, as you look at me as Mother of God suffering the passion with your Son, your whole person is an appeal of love to me from God, "Do whatever he tells you!" You are a firm mother, whose strong love keeps me in the disciplined way of responsible love. For I am your son only if I keep the Lord's commandments. Only thus do I belong to "the rest of the woman's offspring: those who keep the commandments of God and bear testimony to Jesus" (Rev. 12:17).

Hence your concern, Mother, that I do whatever he tells me. Only if I abide in his love by keeping his word am I brother of Jesus and son of God (Mark 3:35), and therefore your son. You speak to me with love's authority! As Mother showing the way, you are ever pointing to Jesus who is the way, the way which you yourself followed, the way of love.

Mary and Social Concern

Mary, not only do you console and strengthen the suffering to carry their burdens, but you are zealous in fighting for the removal of all the unjust burdens which men impose upon one another. You are blessed because you hunger and thirst for justice (Matthew 5:6). Well might we proclaim you patroness of social justice, for you were the first to proclaim your Son's own zeal for justice, as you sang in your Magnificat, "He has scattered the proud in the imagination of their hearts, he has put down the mighty from their thrones and exalted those of low degree; he has filled the hungry with good things, and the rich he has sent empty away!" (Luke 1:51-53).

Through the centuries, the Church in her liturgy on your feast days has always sung the Forty-Fifth Psalm. In this psalm we acclaim your Son as champion of justice: "Ride on triumphant in the cause of truth and for the sake of justice . . . You love justice and hate wickedness" (Psalm 45:4,8). Mary, you see eye to eye with your Son in all his concerns. His concern for the poor and the oppressed has always been your concern. You are a valiant model for all women in our days who are concerned with justice and are filled with compassion for the poor and downtrodden.

You are not simply a quiet and secluded home-maker, providing for the needs of Jesus and Joseph in the little home at Nazareth. The zeal for the poor which you expressed in the Magnificat certainly must have found expression in social concern during your years at Nazareth. Your haste in coming to help your cousin Elizabeth, and your compassion for the embarrassed wedding couple at Cana manifest this concern, and are an inspiration for all women involved in the work of bettering the lot of their fellowmen.

The social problems of our times, especially those which are the cause of suffering for children, can be solved only with the help of concerned women like you. The weighty decisions which have to be made by women in working for a more humane and Christian world are foreshadowed in the world-shaping decision which you made at the Annunciation. There you first carefully pondered God's word, and then, in full freedom, made your decision to commit yourself totally to your Son's work of building a new world in accordance with the Father's will.

All of us in our times, women as well as men, have the responsibility to refashion our world, making it a fitting dwelling place for the sons of God. It is not enough for mothers to be good home-makers. They must be involved in making the whole world a perfect environment for God's children.

Mary, as the valiant woman standing at the cross, you will not let any of us shirk our responsibilities in this regard. As mother of mankind, stir up compassion in our hearts for all our suffering fellowmen. Make us zealous for justice, as you yourself were. Help our women to bring women's viewpoints to bear in reordering a world which is marked so tragically by man's greed and aggressive competition. Fashion your womanly love in the hearts of all women, so that they may bring love's wisdom into the world's order.

Mother, inspire women to begin their work of concern for others in their immediate surroundings. Help them to see that a marriage and a family should never be closed in upon themselves. A home is always part of a larger community, and therefore should be open to the larger community. A woman's influence should reach far beyond her home, and if it does, she and her children and her husband will be all the richer, because she herself will grow in grace and in personality through her devotion to the needs of those around her.

22

PENTECOST AND THE ANNUNCIATION
AS ONE MYSTERY

As type of the Church, Mary, you are not a model of perfection standing above and apart from God's people. You are a member of the Church, and forever one with it. You are the foremost manifestation of the Church's perfection, for in your person the Church is first brought to its perfection. But as one of the redeemed, a member of Adam's race, you always remain a part of the Church. To come into union with the Lord is to come into union with all the people who are the Church, and therefore into union with you, Mary, in your union with the Lord and with his Church.

As one with the Church, you remain ever open with us to the Word and the Spirit of God. You help us to be receptive to the Spirit's continuing work of transforming all of us in your Son's own glory. In you maternal co-operation with the faith of the Church, you are receiving the Holy Spirit of adoption for the children of the Church. You are continuing here and now your role as Mother of Jesus, forming Christ in our hearts.

Thus, the mystery of the Holy Spirit coming upon you at the Annunciation and the mystery of the Holy Spirit coming upon the Church assembled with you in the cenacle at Pentecost (Acts 1:14) are but different aspects of one and the same mystery—the mystery of the Mother of Jesus as one with the whole people of God in receiving the gift of divine life. In the Annunciation we see you, as representative of the whole people of God, praying in perfect openness to God, receiving the Word and Spirit on behalf of us all. In the Pentecost cenacle, we see you praying in the same openness, continuing to receive the Holy Spirit as one with the whole Church.

This Pentecost scene is the last picture given to us in the Scriptures of you in your earthly life. In this scene, you are right in the midst of God's people, very much one with them, and praying in union with them: "All these with one accord devoted themselves to prayer, together with the women and Mary the Mother of Jesus, and with his brothers" (Acts 1:14).

This is a picture of your prayerful presence in the primitive Church, but it also shows your presence in the Church throughout the ages. For God's people do not abandon prayer when they have been taken into heaven. The Scriptures show how the saints in heaven continue to intercede for their brothers and sisters on earth.

In Revelation, the four living creatures and the twenty-four elders fall down before the Lamb "with bowls full of incense, which are the prayers of the saints" (Revelation 5:8). This signifies that the saints in heaven unite their prayers with the prayers of God's people on earth, and offer them to God. The twenty-four elders are saints already in heaven. They offer the prayers of the saints who are still on earth enduring violent persecution.

The saints' heavenly intercession is their way of exercising their share in the Lord's ruling power: "They will be priests of God and of Christ, and will reign with him" (Revelation 20:6). Their priestly share in his kingly reign is the offering of prayers for their brothers on earth who are still fighting the Lord's battle. "The smoke of the incense arose with the prayers of the saints" (Revelation 8:4; see 6:9-11).

Love Inspires Intercession

The saints intercede for us because God's own love, poured out into their hearts by the Holy Spirit whom they possess in fullness, impells them towards us. Mary, just as the Holy Spirit impelled you to hasten to visit Elizabeth to bring the Lord's joy to her, so the saints in heaven are very eager that all of us on earth be filled with their own joy in the Lord, that our joy and theirs may be full.

Knowing that the saints love us and are concerned for us just as you are, Mary, we open our hearts to them in petition, to receive the love and joy they obtain for us from the Lord, to receive the Lord and his Spirit who come to us in this love. Their desire to share with us their own life in the Lord, and their presence with us in the Spirit, awakens in us the hope and the conviction that what they possess can be ours, too. The multitude of the saints is a witness that the outpouring of God's gifts is not limited to a few persons such as you, Mary, but is offered to all mankind. What the Lord has done in the saints manifests what he wishes to do in us, and our hearts expand in hope.

Prayer of petition and prayer of intercession make us receptive to God and his gifts. God forces himself on no one. Petition opens us to him so that he can impart himself to us without imposing himself upon us. God can be received only willingly, in love. Our desire and petition is aroused by God's grace, for only he who is drawn by God in love can come to him (John 6:43). Thus, petition is a means used by God to act upon man, not a means used by man to act upon God. The Spirit himself arouses in us the openness of petition, so that he can fill us (Romans 8:26-27).

Queen of Heaven

Because the Scriptures show that the saints in heaven do not abandon intercession for their brothers and sisters on earth, and are one with Christ who "always lives to make intercession for us" (Hebrews 7:5), the Church has rightly concluded in the Holy Spirit that you, Mary, have not abandoned your maternal mission of intercession and salvation now that you have been assumed into heaven (Vatican II, LG 62). The Church knows this not only from the Scriptures, but through the centuries she has had living experience of it (LG 62:3). Now that the paschal mystery has been completed in you, Mary, you are more powerful on our behalf than you were during your earthly life.

Your share in the power of your Son's priestly reign is in proportion to your share in his whole life on earth, and his battle and victory on the cross. You exercise your queenship on our behalf by your all-powerful intercession, as you continue to pray for us in the midst of the whole communion of saints.

Thus, in a sense, the mysteries of the Annunciation, and of your presence at Pentecost, and of your heavenly Queenship, are but different aspects of the one timeless mystery in which we see you as ever the woman of prayer. In pondering any one of these mysteries as we pray the Rosary, we make ourselves one with you in faith, in receiving Christ and his Holy Spirit into our hearts and our lives.

And by the influence of your maternal presence with us in prayer, you help us open our hearts to these gifts of God. You gently mold our generous response in faith and love. You are the Mother of Christian prayer, and are manifest as such especially at the Annunciation and in the

Pentecost cenacle. The truth expressed in the mystery of your heavenly Queenship is the mystery of the Annunciation and of the Cenacle as timeless, and effective here and now as you continue to pray with us all, in openness to the Holy Spirit as he completes his work in God's people.

Mother of Christian Unity

Rightly, then, Vatican II closes its document on the Church with a picture of you as Mother of Christian Unity. All of God's people on earth and in heaven are gathered together with you in prayer:

> The entire body of the faithful pours forth urgent supplications to the Mother of God and Mother of men, that she who aided the beginnings of the Church by her prayers, may now, exalted as she is above all the angels and saints, intercede before her Son in the fellowship of all the saints, until all families of people, whether they are honored with the title of Christian or whether they still do not know the Savior, may be happily gathered together in peace and harmony into one people of God, for the glory of the most holy and undivided Trinity (LG 69).

My Favorite Marian Mystery

Mother, whether I meditate on you as Queen of Heaven, or as Mother in the Pentecost cenacle, in my heart you are always predominantly the Virgin of the Annunciation, the poor and humble Daughter of Zion praying in hopeful expectation of the Lord. You are closest to me in this scene. I can more easily and truthfully identify with you in the Annunciation than in any other scene, for here I must begin my own spiritual journey. All the power

of your glorious intercession in heaven on my behalf is
fruitless if I do not learn from you first of all to be humble
of heart and obedient to God's word; and yet full of faith,
eager in expectation that the Spirit will overshadow me,
too, and will accomplish wonders in me in the likeness of
what he has done in you.

And yet, though I look upon you as the lowly maiden
when I pray the mystery of your Annunciation, all the
power of your heavenly glory as Queen is with me, for
you are present to me in the power of the Holy Spirit. You
fashion me anew in the likeness of your own lowliness and
your faith at the Annunuciation, not only by the force of
your example, but also by the power of the Holy Spirit,
in whom you are present with me as my mother.

Likewise you are closer to me as Mother at the cross
than as Queen crowned in glory. And yet, because all your
mysteries are timeless, and remain ever present in your
person in your glory, you are the Queen of glory even
when you are present to me in your closeness as Mother
of Sorrows, or your nearness as Virgin of the Annunciation.

That is why in my lowliness or in my sufferings my
predominant attitude in faith and love is always hope and
expectation. For your glory as Queen assumed into heav-
en, and reigning with the Lord, is pledge and promise that
I too will reign in glory with you and your Son. And I
too will sing in glory with you what I now sing with you in
faith on earth:

> My soul proclaims the greatness of the Lord,
> and my spirit exults in God my Savior.
> He has looked upon his lowly handmaid . . .
> The Almighty has done great things for me,
> holy is his name (Luke 1:46).

"Rejoice With Those Who Rejoice"

Mary, though for my sake I love to be with you in the Annunciation, for your sake I love to rejoice with you in your coronation as Queen of Heaven. When I rejoice with you and acclaim you "Blessed" I am fulfilling the Lord's own law of love expressed by St. Paul when he says, "Rejoice with those who rejoice, weep with those who weep" (Romans 12:15). Christ's own love in my heart impells me to rejoice in what he has done in each of my brothers and sisters in the Lord. How then can his love in me fail to rejoice in you, My Mother! I rejoice with you who are transformed in the Lord's glory, and you weep with me, in the sense that you come to my help in my neediness and raise me up to draw me to the Lord. Thus, together we fulfill the law of love.

The Timeless Magnificat

The Book of Revelation shows that the heavenly liturgy consists not just in the saints' intercession for those who are still struggling on earth, but also and especially in their praise of him who sits upon the throne, and of the Lamb in whom we all have the victory. Mary, your hymn of praise in heaven in union with all the saints is but a continuation of the timeless mystery of your Magnificat, your hymn of praise at the Visitation (Luke 1:46-55).

The solo you sang then is now accompanied by the daily chorus of praise sung by the whole people of God, whether on earth or in heaven. Throughout the centuries, the Magnificat has been an invariable part of the Church's official evening liturgy thus continuing perpetually the mystery which began at the Visitation. And as Queen of Heaven you are ever in unison with us, ever in our midst offering with us one hymn of praise.

We praise and thank God even while we offer our petitions and intercessions, for we know that all that we ask for in the name of Jesus, under the inspiration of the Holy Spirit, will most certainly be granted to us as the fruit of the Lamb's sacrifice. Incessantly we offer our praise and thanksgiving to the Lamb and to his Father.

23

THE TIMELESS IMMACULATE
CONCEPTION

Mary, the Fathers of the Church rarely spoke of you without speaking at the same time of the Church, nor did they speak of the Church without speaking of you.[1] Inddeed, frequently they use the same words to describe both you and the Church. For in you as type they saw the reality of the Church already complete, revealing that reality to us.

Isaac of Stella (who died about 1178) summed up this trend of thought of the Fathers, saying, "In the inspired Scriptures, what is said in the widest sense of the Virgin Mother, the Church, is said in a special sense of the Virgin Mary. And what is spoken of the Virgin Mary in a personal way, can rightly be applied in a general way to the Virgin Mother, the Church (ML 194:1863).

That is how it came about in time that the Church, led by the Holy Spirit, began to describe your Immaculate Conception in the same inspired words of Scripture which describe the Church as she will be at her Lord's second coming. Thus, when Pope Pius IX described you as conceived in *spotless* purity and *preserved free* of all sin through the foreseen merits of Jesus *our Savior,* he was using Jude's words about God's people as they will be in their final perfection: "God *our Savior* is able to *preserve you without sin* and to present you *spotless* before the presence of his glory with exceeding joy in the coming of our Lord Jesus Christ" (Jude 24).

We see then, Mary, that the feast of your Immaculate Conception is not simply your personal feast. It is the feast of the whole Church, for you are type and foreshadowing of the immaculate virgin Church. St. Paul speaks of the Church as immaculate, and that is why the Church began to speak of you, her type, as immaculate: "Christ loved the Church and gave himself up for her to make her holy, purifying her in the bath of water by the power of the word, to present to himself a glorious Church, *holy and immaculate,* without stain or wrinkle or anything of that sort" (Ephesians 5:25).

In the second reading for the liturgy for the feast of your Immaculate Conception, St. Paul says to all of God's people: "Before the world was made, God chose us in Christ to be holy and *spotless,* and to live through love *in his presence*" (Ephesians 1:4). In the opening prayer for this feast, we express our faith in the divine teaching concerning your Immaculate Conception, Mary, and pray that God will accomplish his purpose that we, too, will be *sinless in his presence:*

> Father, you prepared the Virgin Mary to be the worthy mother of your Son. You let her share beforehand in the salvation Christ would bring by his death, and kept her sinless from the first moment of her conception. Help us by her prayers to live in your presence without sin.

The mystery of your Immaculate Conception, then, is not just your personal privilege, Mary. It is a privilege in which all of us can share, for the Church in its final glory will be the fulfillment of the history which began in your conception in the womb of your mother, Ann. Speaking of you as type of the Church, Vatican II says: "While in the most holy Virgin the Church has already reached that perfection whereby she is without spot and wrinkle, the followers of Christ still strive to increase in holiness by conquering sin" (LG 65).

The word "immaculate" sums up the mystery of every Christian's spiritual life. Or better still, Mary, God reveals in you, the one whom he has created immaculate, what he expects our spiritual life to be, and what he wills to make it be. We are members of the Church, and in each of us the Church's mystery must be accomplished. This mystery begins with you, Mary Immaculate, and we in our turn, by the power of the Holy Spirit, must become immaculate in the Blood of the Redeemer.

In each of us, the victory over the serpent must be achieved. Foretold in the woman of Genesis 3:15, Christ first fully accomplished this victory in you, Mary: "The Lord God said to the serpent: I will put enmity between you and the woman, and between your seed and her seed; he shall bruise your head, and you shall bruise his heel" (Genesis 3:15). What the Lord first accomplished in you, Mary, he is now bringing about in us, for Paul says to all of God's people, "The God of peace will quickly crush Satan under your feet" (Romans 16:20).

Your Immaculate Conception is God's promise and pledge to us that the victory will be our through Christ, his Son and your Son, this Jesus "who by the eternal Spirit offered himself immaculate to God" (Hebrews 9:14). Christ has "reconciled you in his body of flesh by his death, to present you holy and immaculate and blameless before him" (Colossians 1:22).

Therefore in the preface of the Eucharistic Prayer for the feast of your Immaculate Conception, we praise and thank God our Father, saying:

You allowed no stain of Adam's sin to touch the Virgin Mary. Full of grace, she was to be a worthy mother of your Son. She was your sign of favor to the Church at its beginning, and the promise of its final perfection as the Bride of Christ, radiant in beauty. Purest of virgins, she was to bring forth your Son, the innocent Lamb who takes away our sins. You chose her from all women to be your gift to your people, our advocate with you and our pattern of holiness. O Mary, conceived without sin, pray for us who have recourse to you!

24

AN INFANT'S JOY

O Jesus, Son of God, now I know why you came to us in the womb of a woman, Mary, the mother of love! At the sound of Mary's voice in greeting her cousin Elizabeth, the infant John in Elizabeth's womb leapt for joy. I know now the significance of that infant's joy, now that I have come to realize that many an infant even in his mother's womb has the beginnings of fear and sorrow.

Long before we have eyes to see and ears to hear, we are already receiving sensations through the nerves which develop in us when we are but an embryo or fetus in our mother's womb. Though most children are lovingly received by the mothers who conceive them, many children are unwanted. An unwanted child in his mother's womb already senses that he is unwanted, even before his sense of touch has developed. For his nerves are already responding to the nerves of his mother's body. If she resents his presence in her womb, he feels this in all the fibres of his being, and he reacts with an incipient fear of the very one who should be loving and cherishing him.

But when a mother welcomes the infant in her womb with great joy, then this love and joy is communicated to the infant. He is therefore ready to come into the world in joy, trusting in his mother and responding to her love.

When a mother does not want her child, in many cases it is because he is a threat to her ease and comfort, and it will cost her something to bear him and nurture him. She thinks that he is a burden, and thus she makes him a burden instead of a joy. And her own sin of un-lovingness, her unwillingness to go out of her self-centered-ness to love the child, is communicated to him by the re-sentful fibres of her nervous system. And the fibres of his being react, resenting this lack of love and acceptance. His whole nature was created for love—to be loved and to love—but he starts life unloved and unloving!

Is not this one of the ways in which original sin, the sin of the generations which have preceded us, can be passed on to us even in our mother's womb? The sin of our "first parents" is transmitted to us in the sins of our more immediate parents, and we in turn ratify it. Thus, the child who is already fearful and resentful in his moth-er's womb is likely someday to accept consciously and ratify willingly this resentment, which at first is but the spontaneous reaction of the nerve fibres of his sense life. He is likely to turn the resentment into sin when he comes to the use of reason by consenting to it and turning it into a willful act of rejection of those who have rejected him. And thus he too will become a full-fledged sinner like those who have sinned against him.

And even if his immediate parents have never re-sented or rejected him, but have lovingly and joyfully re-ceived him, the whole human society into which he is born is only too often like a hostile womb. This he learns to resent, unless he is lovingly received in a loving commu-nity. He is sinned against in many ways in a hostile, sin-ning world. Others use him for their own selfish purposes. Greed and injustice often deprive him of his rights and needs. The sins of others wound and scar him repeatedly. And ever so many of his own sins stem from his resentment of those who have sinned against him.

As Jesus carries his cross, he alludes to a prophecy of Hosea, saying, "Blessed are the barren and the wombs that never bore, and the breasts that never gave suck" (Luke 23:29; Cf. Hosea 9:11-17). These words seem to say that it is a greater blessing not to have children than to have them. All the joy of childbearing can be turned into bitterness when a mother sees how her sons and daughters are sinned against, and how they become sinners in turn by reacting against those who have sinned against them.

O Jesus! The joy of the infant John as he leaps in his mother's womb at your coming is a sign that all this sorrow has been reversed and turned to joy. For you have come to us in the loving womb of Mary, the generous womb which so willingly accepted you from the Father's bosom. When Luke tells us of the wonderful joy which your mother brings to the home of Elizabeth, he is telling us that in the womb of Mary all the curse and sorrow of sin and death is turned into blessing and joy and life!

Lord Jesus, you echoed the prophecy of Hosea when you said, "Blessed are the barren and the wombs that never bore, and the breasts that never gave suck" (Luke 23:29; Hosea 9:14). The reversal of this prophecy is announced in the prophetic words of the woman who cried out from the crowd, "Blessed is the womb that bore you, and the breasts that you sucked" (Luke 11:27).

O Mary, "blessed are you among women, and blessed is the fruit of your womb!" (Luke 1:42). The curse of sin is removed in the birthpangs endured by Jesus on the cross, and by your sharing in those birthpangs, and so our joy is made full. You brought forth your Son in joy, a joy which is completed in our joy in our redemption.

The blessed fruit of your womb destroys the curses

pronounced in Genesis. Elizabeth's joy in bearing John shows that the decree pronounced over Eve—"in pain you shall bring forth children" (Genesis 3:16) — has been cancelled. For the pains of childbirth are but the symbol of the miseries of the world of sin into which we are born. But when these miseries are suffered in union with Jesus, the blessed "new man" is born. Jesus, the fruit of your womb, takes away sin, and therefore removes the curse of the misery entailed by sin.

Is it any wonder, Mary, that Christian tradition has seen in your immaculate holiness the beginnings of the new creation which is free from all sin! The old creation, under the curse of sin, has become a new creation in Christ, filled with blessings. "Behold I make all things new!" (Revelation 21:5). Mary and Jesus, Elizabeth and John, you are the promise and pledge of recreation for all of us!

Blessed are those who have never experienced a resentful womb, but have been received by their mothers with great love and joy! Every mother who welcomes her child in love finds wonderful new cause for joy when she ponders the mystery of the Visitation and sees you coming, Mary, with the infant Jesus in your womb, and the joy he brings to Elizabeth and her infant John. In the sheer joy of pregnancy the Christian mother cries out, "I am flooded with God's goodness and power at work within me. And because Jesus came to me in a mother's womb, my child, after he has been born of me, will be born again of water and the Holy Spirit in baptism, the womb of Mother Church. He can be child not only of man and woman, but son of God in Jesus, the beloved Son!"

25

MY "IMMACULATE CONCEPTION"

Now I understand why we celebrate your Immaculate Conception, O Mary conceived without sin! There is an immaculate conception promised for each one of us. When I accept God's love poured out to me in the person of Jesus whom you once carried in your womb, in faith I am conceived anew of spotless love, conceived anew immaculately as I respond lovingly to love. I am born anew of God and his Holy Spirit of love.

And the healing power of your redemption, O Jesus, reaches back to my very origins in my mother's womb, healing me of the resentments and rebellions I may have experienced against that womb, or against the home and the world into which I was born. I may never have resented my parents or my home, for these may have received me with great love and joy. But perhaps I have been injured and rejected by others in this sinful world, and in turn I may have sinned against them. But your redeeming power, O Jesus, heals me of all the wounds I may have received from others, and of the wounds I have inflicted upon myself by my resentments against those who have injured me.

Thus by your redeeming power, Lord, I can start life anew in purity and holiness. Your light and your grace help me to recognize and renounce all these reactions

158

against those who have not loved me, all those sins I have committed by consenting to the spontaneous reactions of my wounded being. Your love, Jesus, and Mary's love have replaced the unloving womb of this hostile world. And in your love, brought to me in your mother's love, and in the love of all who love me, I am healed by loving in return, loving and forgiving those who have rejected me.

Even now that I am old and grey, Lord, you can reach back, as it were, even into my mother's womb if necessary, and into my childhood and adolescence and maturity, taking away from my heart all the resentments by which I may have responded to lack of love. By the power of your prayer on the cross, "Father, forgive them, for they know not what they do" (Luke 23:24), I can forgive those who have not loved me, and can be forgiven my own failure to love.

If by faith and baptism I was conceived anew in the loving womb of Mother Church, the complete healing of my wounds which I may have received in an unloving world can take place only if I am kept in this womb of love; that is, only in the Christian community of love can all my human relationships be healed in love. If my sin consists in reacting to and rejecting the unloving ones around me, my healing consists in my loving response to love, and my loving forgiveness of all who have not loved me. The very ones who have not loved me are healed of unlove when my love reaches out to them, and they respond in love. All this is possible because God's own love is poured out into our hearts by the Holy Spirit who is given to us (Romans 5:5).

Thus my healing, begun in Baptism, reaches back to the wounds which began in me in my mother's womb, so

that at last I am immaculate even as far back as my conception, when all my resentments and fears and lack of
love are replaced with love and joy and communion. Lord,
you who were with me in love, fashioning me in my mother's womb, are able to restore all that may have been un-
done in that womb and in the rest of my life. "Truly, you
have formed my inmost being; you knit me together in
my mother's womb" (Psalm 139:13). For those who love
you, you transform all things into good (Romans 8:28)—
even my sins of the past—as your love in me changes my
resentments and rejection and sins into loving acceptance
and forgiveness.

Of course, Mary, the healing of all my wounds and
sinfulness is not quite the same as your unique preservation, by the redeeming grace of your Son, from all sin
and wounds even in the instant of your conception. In
the Prayer After the Communion on the Feast of your Immaculate Conception, we pray for this healing which is
pledged to us in your preservation from sin: "Lord God,
by a unique privilege you preserved Our Lady from all
sin. Grant that this Eucharist which we have received may
heal the wounds which sin has inflicted on us."

Though I may have sinned in many ways through
unfaithfulness to the Lord, your whole person as the immaculate one, Mary, reveals to me that, in the blood of
the Lamb, I can be reborn in virginal purity. The Lord
can recreate me holy and spotless (Ephesians 5:26-27).
My failures in the past do not destroy my hope for the fu-
ture. "Fear not, O Zion, do not be discouraged. The Lord,
your God, is in your midst, a mighty savior; he will rejoice over you with gladness, and renew you in his love"
(Zephaniah 3:16).

"Knit Together in Love"

It is love for one another and for all men which makes us immaculate and holy for the coming of the Bridegroom: "May the Lord make you increase and abound in love for one another and for all men, as we do for you, so that he may establish your hearts unblameable in holiness before our God and Father at the coming of our Lord Jesus Christ with all the saints" (1 Thess. 3:12-13).

It is not this act of love or that one, it is not feeding this hungry person or clothing that naked one (Matt. 25:35) which prepares us for the Bridegroom at his coming. We are ready to receive the Lord only when our whole life and all our human relationships are integrated in love. Our baptismal purity has to be expressed in the purity of our love for one another: "Having purified your souls by your obedience to the truth for a sincere love of the brethren, love one another earnestly from the heart" (1 Peter 1:22).

Thus, Immaculate Mary, as type of the Church, you are a symbol of the people who "knit together in love" (Colossians 2:2), in communion with God in communion with one another. Your Immaculate Heart, filled with love for God and for mankind, is the symbol of the unity of all God's people in love.

26

MARY AND THE HOLY TRINITY

The three divine Persons of the Blessed Trinity, Father, Son and Holy Spirit, are sometimes depicted with Mary, the Mother of Jesus, in their midst. In this way, two key mysteries of the Christian faith are expressed: the mystery of Mary as type of God's people, and the mystery of God's people invited into the very heart of the Holy Trinity. These two mysteries are one.

O Mary, already present with your Son in the bosom of the Father, help me to enlighten my readers concerning this mystery, the mystery of the ultimate fulfillment of the paschal mystery of Jesus. In this fulfillment, all of us, together with you, will dwell in the very life of the three divine Persons, sharing in the wedding feast of the Lamb.

The Roublev Ikon

The Roublev Ikon of the Most Holy Trinity is a magnificent expression of the meaning of the Holy Trinity in the life of Christians. Like every good ikon, this one expresses a timeless mystery. Eternity and events of time are represented simultaneously, in such a way that the beholder of the ikon is made contemporary with the whole mystery and every facet of it: its eternal beginnings, its aspects which develop in time, and its ultimate fulfillment in the eternity in which it began.

This ikon shows forth the mystery of the Holy Trinity and the paschal mystery of the Lamb as somehow one eternal mystery; namely, the mystery of mankind brought through Christ into the very life of the three divine Persons.

The ikon represents a meal, and the meal takes palce in heaven and on earth. The setting of the scene is on earth, for the three divine Persons are represented as the three angels who visited Abraham and accepted his hospitality (Genesis 18). Yet the action takes place in eternity. For the scene depicts the eternal decision of the Son of God to accept the Father's decision to send him into the world, to be the paschal Lamb sacrificed for our salvation.

But the scene also evokes the Last Supper, and every Eucharistic celebration, for on closer inspection we see that in the wine in the cup on the table, there is a figure of "the Lamb who has been slain from the foundation of the world" (Revelation 13:8).

The outlines of the figures of the three Persons form a circle, symbolizing the perfect, intimate, loving communion of the three divine Persons. The very postures of the three express eloquently their pouring out of self to one another in love. The circular movement of love goes from the figure at the right, through the central figure, into the one at the left. The Spirit who is love is poured out in the Father's love for the Son, and in the Son's love for the Father.

The three are seated at table, signifying that their very life is eternally nourished by their self-giving to each other. This loving communion, which is their very life, is the heavenly banquet.

A cross is suggested within the circle of the divine communion by the halos of the three figures; for the central halo, against the vertical line of the tree of life, is a little higher than the horizontal line between the two outer halos. The cross is an integral element in the loving communion of the Three, for their communion is eternally perfected in their mutual total self-giving to one another. Each of the Persons is unmindful of self and totally intent on the other.

The ikon depicts the decisions to make the cross a self-giving to mankind as well as a self-giving within the divine life. For the central figure is the Father, pointing to the cup, proposing to the One sitting at his right hand that he drink this cup of suffering. The Son, returning the Father's look, gazes into his eyes with a trace of sadness, the sadness which will overwhelm the Son in the agony in the garden. But his hand is already reaching out to take the cup. The fingers of his hand are extended in the manner in which a priest of the Eastern Church bestows a blessing. He is blessing the cup, consecrating it for us as our Eucharistic drink. Thus, without leaving the eternal moment of the Son's decision to come to earth, we are present at the Last Supper.

The Father's fingers, too, are extended in readiness to bless what the Son blesses, blessing mankind with the fruits of the paschal mystery, the wine of the Holy Spirit. The tree of life behind the Father, identified with the vertical beam of the eternal cross of love, is once again life-giving for men through the blood of the Lamb in the Cup.

The third Person, in eager expectancy, is looking at the cup, in readiness to bring its contents to all for whom it will be shed. His eyes are looking towards the Son as they are looking at the cup, awaiting the Son's action which must precede his own. He is poised in loving eagerness to pour himself out to mankind in the blood of the Lamb, for in the blood, the life-giving Spirit gives himself and is sent to all who believe in the Lamb.

Even the Mother of Jesus is in the picture. For the building behind the figure of the Son represents the New Jerusalem, the Church. Since Mary is type of the Church and one with it, the church building in the picture fittingly symbolizes Mary herself, who continues her maternity as one with the Church's maternity. The part of the building extending out over the head of the Son symbolizes Mary's protective love, covering her Son and all who will become one with him through his blood and Spirit.

Eternity, Eden, Abraham, Last Supper, Calvary, Pentecost, each Eucharistic celebration, the Mother of Jesus, the Church—all these are superimposed in the one ikon, and are made simultaneously present to the beholder.

But that is not all. Even while the beholder looks back to the eternal decision of the three divine Persons to send the Lamb to be slain, and, in his Blood, to pour out the Holy Spirit of love into the hearts of believers; and even while he hears the Son say, as he comes into the world, "Behold I come to do your will, O God" (Hebrews 10:5); and even while he sees the Last Supper in progression; at the same time, and especially, he is looking ahead to the ultimate eternal fulfillment of this one magnificent mystery.

For at the table around which the three figures are sitting, there is an open space, a fourth place. There is room for a guest at the heavenly banquet, the inner communion which is the very life of the Three.

And the invited guest is the Church, the people of God, who are all called to full communion in the life of the three divine Persons. Just as the eternal nourishment of the Three is their loving, life-giving communion with one another, so the banquet of the Lamb to which mankind is invited is this same nourishment, now given to God's people who are brought into this communion.

The beholder of the ikon is the Church, God's people, hearing the invitation to the banquet of life.

O Mother Mary, the Church has already accepted this invitation through the consent which you gave at the Annunciation. And in your person as Queen of Heaven, the Church is already seated at the heavenly banquet.

Your consent at the Annunciation, Mary, is simultaneous with the Lamb's action in carrying out the consent he gave to the eternal decision to send him into the world. Your "Behold the handmaid of the Lord" (Luke 1:38) coincides with his "Behold I come to do your will, O God" as he enters into the world (Hebrews 10:5). Through your consent which coincides with his, Mary, the wedding of the Lamb with mankind is contracted.

This is a wedding banquet, and the guest is the Bride! "And I saw the holy city, New Jerusalem, coming down out of heaven from God, prepared as a bride adorned for her husband" (Revelation 21:2). "Blessed are those who are invited to the marriage supper of the Lamb" (Revelation 19:9).

"Behold, I stand at the door and knock; if anyone hears my voice and opens the door, I will come in to him and eat with him, and he with me" (Revelation 3:20).

27

THE MOTHER OF JESUS WAS THERE

Mother, were I a gifted ikon artist, I believe I would copy Andrew Roublev's ikon of the Holy Trinity, but would then fill in the fourth place at the table with your figure. But rather than have you face only the three divine Persons at the table, I would have you turned towards us, inviting us to the banquet which you are enjoying. Using the words with which John begins the story of the wedding at Cana, I would entitle my ikon, "The Mother of Jesus was there" (John 2:1).

For the heavenly banquet is a wedding feast, too. It is the wedding feast of the Lamb, at which he is united with his bride, the Church. The heavenly feast is the fulfillment of the paschal mystery in all its phases, whether in its beginnings on earth, or in its completion in heaven. And therefore, too, Mary, you are inseparable from every Eucharistic celebration of this mystery. That is why the Church has always remembered you by name in the Eucharistic Prayer, mentioning you along with the whole communion of saints, all of whom are somehow united with every Eucharistic celebration, for they are all the Body of Christ.

Likewise, Mary, you are inseparable from Mother Church whenever and wherever she preaches the gospel, inviting all of us to the heavenly banquet: "Come, for all is now ready!" (Luke 14:17; Proverbs 9:1-6). Your role at Cana, preparing the disciples for faith in Jesus, is continued by the Church as she preaches the faith, and you continue your Cana role in and with the Church.

All of this I would express in my ikon, showing you at the heavenly table as type of the Church, and yet turned towards us, calling us, too, to the heavenly banquet. Even while you yourself are in full communion with the three divine Persons in the eternal circle of love, you are ever turned also towards us, drawing us into this communion.

Intimacy and Openness

The Lord himself at the Last Supper said that it should be so. For he taught that all who are in communion with him and the Father must live in communion with one another, and must ever be intent on bringing others into this same communion: "That they may all be one; even as you, Father, are in me, and I in you, that they also may be in us, so that the world may believe that you have sent me . . . and have loved them even as you have loved me" (John 17:21,23).

The fraternal love of the disciples of Jesus is a sharing in the divine love in which the divine Persons eternally respond to one another in perfect communion with each other: "that the love with which you have loved me may be in them, and I in them" (John 17:26). Love in its perfection is essentially communion. Father and Son are united in the Holy Spirit in absolute intimacy and perfect communion. Infinitely open to each other, they are infinitely self-giving to each other. The circle of their intimate communion is complete and perfect in itself.

Nevertheless, in a gesture of totally gratuitous generosity (expressed so beautifully in the gestures of all three figures in the Roublev ikon), God has willed to open this intimacy of the divine communion. Thus, in Jesus, God's love is revealed as perfect communion in complete intimacy, and at the same time as openness without limits.

If that is the very structure of divine love within the Trinity, that is how this love operates in the community of the children of God, born of water and the Spirit and gathered together in the blood of the Lamb. This Christian love is simultaneously intimate communion and perfect openness. It is intimate communion with the divine Persons and with one another, and it is openness to all the rest of mankind. It can never be wrapped up in itself, in indifference to the world. By reason of its source in the Trinity, it is always open communion. It is open to others precisely because it is intimate communion in the life of the Three. God is total intimacy and total openness—and so is the Church!

The role of those who are already in full communion with the three divine Persons in inviting others into this communion is the essential role of the Church. This role is personified and fulfilled to perfection in you, Mary, who carry out this role in a superlative way.

In the Roublev ikon, the intimate communion of the three Persons is so open to the expected guest, that the whole topic of the dinner conversation, in which they are expressing their communion with one another, is their preparations for the guest, the Bride of the Lamb. She is to be washed and made spotless in the Blood of the Lamb (Ephesians 5:25-27).

And the Three expect this same communion and openness of all who accept the invitation to the table. That is why you, Mary, taken into the glory of God in your assumption, seated at the heavenly feast and wholly caught up into the intimacy of the three divine Persons, are nevertheless ever turning towards us, drawing us into this same intimate communion with God.

Mary, our sister and our mother, to call you Daughter of the eternal Father, Mother of the eternal Son, Spouse of the eternal Spirit, is not to make you God, "fourth person of the Blessed Trinity," but is to express your wonderful relationships with each of the three divine Persons, your intimate communion with them, the communion into which all of us are called. You are already within that perfect circle, which is open to all of us. Your presence in the midst of the Three is promise and pledge that all of us shall someday join you there, through Christ, your Son and the Father's.

"The Mother of Jesus was there" while this book was being written. Mother, be there whenever and wherever it is read. Through its words, carry on your own role as Mother of Faith and Mother of Jesus in us, for the glory of the holy undivided Trinity, Father, Son, and Holy Spirit! Amen!